S0-AJM-342

Dean A. Wilkening

Ballistic-Missile Defence
and Strategic Stability

WITHDRAWN

Adelphi Paper 334

COLORADO COLLEGE LIBRARY
COLORADO SPRINGS
COLORADO

Oxford University Press, Great Clarendon Street, Oxford OX2 6DP
Oxford New York
Athens Auckland Bangkok Bombay Calcutta Cape Town
Dar es Salaam Delhi Florence Hong Kong Istanbul Karachi
Kuala Lumpur Madras Madrid Melbourne Mexico City
Nairobi Paris Singapore Taipei Tokyo Toronto
and associated companies in
Berlin Ibadan

Oxford is a trade mark of Oxford University Press

Published in the United States
by Oxford University Press Inc., New York

© The International Institute for Strategic Studies 2000

First published May 2000 by **Oxford University Press** for
The International Institute for Strategic Studies
Arundel House, 13–15 Arundel Street, Temple Place, London WC2R 3DX

Director John Chipman
Editor Mats R. Berdal
Assistant Editor Matthew Foley
Project Manager, Design and Production Mark Taylor

All rights reserved. No part of this publication may be reproduced, stored in a
retrieval system or transmitted in any form or by any means, electronic, mechanical
or photo-copying, recording or otherwise, without the prior permission of The
International Institute for Strategic Studies. Within the UK, exceptions are allowed
in respect of any fair dealing for the purpose of research or private study, or
criticism or review, as permitted under the Copyright, Designs and Patents Act,
1988, or in the case of reprographic reproduction in accordance with the terms of
the licences issued by the Copyright Licensing Agency. Enquiries concerning
reproduction outside these terms and in other countries should be sent c/o
Permissions, Journals Department, Oxford University Press, Great Clarendon
Street, Oxford, OX2 6DP, UK.

This book is sold subject to the condition that it shall not, by way of trade or
otherwise, be lent, re-sold, hired out or otherwise circulated without the
publisher's prior consent in any form of binding or cover other than that in which it
is published and without a similar condition including this condition being
imposed on the subsequent purchaser.

British Library Cataloguing in Publication Data
Data available

Library of Congress Cataloguing in Publication Data

ISBN 0-19-929004-0
ISSN 0567-932x

UG
743
.W54
2000

Contents

Introduction

Over the next decade, the US will deploy theatre-missile defences and, possibly, a limited national missile defence. This will have wide-ranging effects. If they work, these systems will protect US troops, allies and the American homeland from emerging ballistic-missile threats. In the long term, however, their deployment could undermine US security by damaging relations with Russia and China, and by placing major new strains on relations with key allies in Europe. At worst, reductions in US and Russian strategic nuclear forces could cease, and both Moscow and Beijing could engage in a renewed arms race. This would undermine efforts to limit the proliferation of ballistic missiles and weapons of mass destruction. If theatre-defence systems are deployed to Taiwan, the US could even find itself at war with China.

Political pressure has nonetheless grown in the US for the further development and early deployment of defensive systems. This has given rise to the third American debate on ballistic-missile defence (BMD) since the 1960s. The first of these culminated in the signing of the Anti-Ballistic Missile (ABM) Treaty in 1972. The treaty, a cornerstone of Cold War strategic arms control, is in its existing form incompatible with current US plans for national missile defence. In the 1980s, President Ronald Reagan's Strategic Defense Initiative sparked the second US debate on BMD, which centred on the feasibility and advisability of developing a defensive 'shield' against Soviet threats to the US homeland. Although the so-called 'Stars Wars' programme was never formally abandoned, the end of the Cold War ensured that its ambitious scale was reduced, and that the heated debate surrounding its merits died down. Many of the earlier arguments in favour of deploying defensive systems, as well as the principal objections, have resurfaced in the third debate, which is now under way. Advocates claim that the proposed systems are essential to US security, and should be deployed as soon as possible, regardless of the ABM Treaty. Critics argue that they upset strategic stability, encourage regional arms races, and will not in any case work. But the context and character of the current BMD debate differ from those of its predecessors in important respects. Two features in particular stand out.

First, the nature of the threat has changed. Behind the pressure for early deployment lies a growing concern about the proliferation of missiles and related technology to so-called 'rogue' states, most prominently North Korea, Iran and Iraq. The acquisition by these states of missiles able to deliver nuclear, biological or chemical (NBC) weapons is seen as posing an increasingly credible threat to US allies, to US military forces stationed abroad, and even to the American homeland. The need to protect against an accidental or unauthorised ballistic-missile launch by Russia, or perhaps China, is considered a matter of less pressing, albeit still genuine, concern.

Second, unlike the Cold War debates on BMD, a broad bipartisan consensus has developed within the US political establishment in support of the basic idea that deploying missile defences, if handled properly, is likely to enhance rather than diminish US security. Although there have been dissenting voices, both presidential candidates for the November 2000 elections have declared their support for missile defences, and there is solid support within Congress for deployment. Several European countries have reluctantly, and in some cases with privately expressed misgivings, come to recognise the depth of US feeling on this issue. Barring a major technological setback in the near future, the question increasingly appears to be not whether the US will deploy BMD, but when it will do so, and what kinds of systems it will choose.

This paper is concerned with the wider impact of the likely deployment of US national and theatre-missile defences during the first decade of the twenty-first century. It draws upon detailed quantitative analysis to assess the possible consequences of deploying:

- a limited national missile-defence system designed to protect the US against small accidental or unauthorised attacks by Russia, or accidental, unauthorised or intentional attacks by other states to which intercontinental ballistic missiles (ICBMs) might proliferate; and
- theatre-missile defences aimed at protecting allied cities and US troops from theatre-range missiles armed with NBC weapons.

The central question this paper poses is what level of national and theatre defence would be sufficient to meet these objectives, without appearing threatening to the other nuclear powers, and without undermining regional stability in areas of major interest to the US and its allies. Answering this question means assessing the perform-ance levels that BMD systems must meet to be considered 'effective'. It also requires a closer look at why the US is seeking these defences, as well as at some of the possible reactions to their deployment from potential adversaries. These may include 'technical' responses, such as deploying more missiles or developing countermeasures aimed at defeating BMD systems. American BMD deployments may also encourage more far-reaching political and strategic realignments among the major powers.

This paper argues that there is no immediate need to deploy US national missile defences because accidental and unauthorised Russian or Chinese attacks are unlikely, and because deterrence should mean that the risk of attack from emerging ballistic-missile states is acceptably low. If US leaders fear that deterrence might fail, the US could launch pre-emptive conventional strikes to destroy fixed missile sites. National missile defence might be a useful insurance against small accidental or unauthorised attacks, the failure of deterrence or ineffective counterforce attacks, but other defence needs are more pressing. However, if such a system were deployed, modifying the ABM Treaty to allow the US and Russia to deploy up to 100 interceptors at multiple sites around their territory should not pose a realistic threat to the retaliatory capabilities of four of the five declared nuclear powers. A 100-interceptor system would, however, eliminate China's current strategic retaliatory capability against the US. It is therefore clear that deploying even a relatively modest national missile defence will have the most direct impact on China's strategic capability.

The proliferation of theatre-range ballistic missiles is a more pressing problem. Assuming they work, current US programmes provide for enough interceptors to handle plausible regional threats. However, these systems have yet to prove themselves effective on the test range against potential countermeasures. Few counter-measures exist against boost-phase BMD systems (which destroy missile boosters, rather than warheads). Specifically, airborne boost-phase interceptors may be an effective choice for theatre-missile defence, as well as for protecting the US homeland against ICBMs launched from small emerging ballistic-missile states such as North Korea. Moreover, an airborne boost-phase defence would pose very little threat to the strategic forces of the five major nuclear powers. With the exception of accidental or unauthorised Russian or Chinese launches, airborne systems may therefore provide the most effective theatre *and* national missile defence – without upsetting strategic stability.

Chapter 1

Ballistic-Missile Proliferation

Assessing the Threat

The proliferation of ballistic missiles is of concern because their modest payloads, short attack times, and the current lack of adequate defences make them attractive for delivering NBC weapons. Although the relatively poor accuracy of indigenously produced missiles in emerging ballistic-missile states makes them militarily ineffectual for conventional attacks, it does not appreciably reduce their effectiveness for delivering NBC weapons against large military facilities or urban targets.[1] The military impact of conventionally armed ballistic missiles lies in their ability to divert a significant portion of the defender's air forces as it attempts to locate and destroy the missile launchers. The amount of actual damage they can inflict is sufficiently small that substantial efforts, including deploying ballistic-missile defences, are probably not justified if this is the only threat one faces.

Aside from the five declared nuclear powers, about 25 states either have, or are trying to acquire, ballistic missiles (see Appendix 1, page 75). North Korea, Iran, Iraq and perhaps Syria and Libya pose the most serious threats because of their modest ballistic-missile capabilities, coupled with their antagonism towards the US or its allies. North Korea is particularly troublesome because it has sold ballistic-missile technologies and production facilities, as well as fully assembled missiles, abroad. Most proliferation to date has involved short-range ballistic missiles (SRBMs). In the next five years, medium-range ballistic missiles (MRBMs) will be deployed.

North Korea's *No-dong* 1 is thought to be operational already, while the two-stage *Taepo-dong* 1 was first flight-tested on 31 August 1998, with a solid rocket third stage that attempted to place a small (15 kilogram) satellite into low-earth orbit. Pakistan's *Ghauri*, which is based on the *No-dong*, was flight-tested for the first time in April 1998, and again in April 1999. Iran's *Shahab*-3 MRBM, also based on *No-dong* technology, was first flight-tested in July 1998; it too may be operational.[2] Finally, India tested its *Agni* 2 MRBM in April 1999. Reasonable estimates of the number of MRBMs in emerging arsenals, at least for the next decade, are between 50 and 200 missiles. Intermediate-range ballistic missiles (IRBMs) and ICBMs may also appear, although they require larger engines and multi-stage missiles. North Korea's *Taepo-dong* 1 launch demonstrated that Pyongyang had succeeded in missile staging.[3]

Several states have also shown interest in the lucrative satellite-launch business, which requires large multistage rockets, many components of which are common to ICBMs. While significant differences exist between the two (space-launch vehicles have lighter structural weights, vernier rocket motors for orbit injection and, usually, non-storable propellants), sufficient overlap exists so that a state which has mastered space-launch technology can probably master ICBMs fairly quickly. Space-launch vehicles themselves could be used to deliver NBC warheads over intercontinental ranges, although they cannot be considered survivable military missiles. Besides the five major nuclear powers, Japan, Brazil, India, Israel and Ukraine have active space-launch-vehicle programmes, while North Korea and Iran intend to develop them.[4]

Russia and China are the only two countries currently fielding ICBMs that could pose a threat to the US homeland. A controversial US National Intelligence Estimate in 1995 stated that no new ballistic-missile threat would appear to the continental United States before 2010.[5] However, an assessment by an independent commission headed by former Secretary of Defense Donald H. Rumsfeld in 1998 stated that the threats to the US were 'broader, more mature, and emerging more rapidly' than previous intelligence estimates had suggested; that such threats might appear 'within about five years of a decision to acquire such a capability' by states such as North Korea and Iran, or ten years in the case of Iraq; and that 'the [US] intelligence community's ability to provide timely and accurate estimates of ballistic missile threats to the US is eroding'.[6] In particular, little warning may precede operational deployments.

The Rumsfeld report portrayed a more serious ballistic-missile threat for three reasons. It did not assume that emerging ballistic-missile states would require the same high standards for accuracy, reliability and safety that characterise US and former-Soviet programmes, nor would they necessarily seek large arsenals. It assumed that extensive technical assistance from outside sources was readily available, notwithstanding the Missile Technology Control Regime (MTCR), and that countries were increasingly able to conceal important parts of their ballistic-missile programmes.[7] Despite initial disagreement, the US intelligence community now substantially endorses the commission's findings. A report by the National Intelligence Council in September 1999 claimed that North Korea 'probably will test' the *Taepo-dong* 2 IRBM by 2001, unless delayed for political reasons. The report also assessed that Iran is 'likely to test' a space-launch vehicle, which could be converted into an ICBM, by 2010, and that Iraq may test an ICBM before 2015. The extent of foreign assistance is the greatest single factor that could move this timetable forward.[8]

If countries other than Russia and China develop ICBM capabilities by 2010, they are unlikely to deploy more than a few liquid-fuel missiles based at relatively vulnerable fixed sites. Solid-fuel mobile ICBMs are beyond the reach of emerging ballistic-missile states for the foreseeable future. The first Russian solid-fuel ICBM (the SS-13) lagged behind the development of first-generation liquid-fuel ICBMs by approximately ten years. This was also the case for third-generation missiles, such as the liquid-fuel SS-18 and SS-19, and the solid-fuel SS-24 and SS-25. China took approximately 20 years between deploying the first DF-5 liquid-fuel ICBM, and the first flight test of a solid-fuel ICBM (the DF-31, in August 1999). China built an ICBM force containing only approximately 20 silo-based, liquid-fuel ICBMs during its first 35 years as a nuclear power.

North Korea is the first emerging ballistic-missile state likely to develop an ICBM capability. With a range estimated at between 4,000km and 6,000km, the *Taepo-dong* 2 could strike parts of Alaska or the western tip of Hawaii with a 1,000kg payload. Adding a third stage would allow a payload of 200–300kg to be delivered anywhere within the continental United States.[9] Iran is also believed to have an active ICBM programme enjoying substantial assistance from Russia, China and North Korea.[10] Although the UN Special Commission (UNSCOM) largely dismantled Iraq's capacity to produce missiles with ranges of over 150km, the Rumsfeld Commission concluded that Baghdad could reconstitute a long-range ballistic-missile programme within ten years because the expertise and some of the equipment still exists in the country.[11] India and Pakistan are also engaged in long-range missile programmes, but these countries are less likely to come into conflict with the US.

Consequently, the problem of ballistic-missile proliferation in the short term concerns the spread to states hostile to the US of NBC-armed missiles with ranges of less than approximately 4,000km. This poses a growing threat to US troops overseas, and to US allies. The threat to the US homeland consists of the possibility that a third stage could be added to intermediate-range missiles, thereby creating an ICBM with a delivery capability of several hundred kilograms – sufficient for biological and chemical warheads, and perhaps for a single first-generation nuclear warhead.[12] There is also the possibility, however remote, of an accidental or unauthorised ballistic-missile launch by Russia or China, or indeed any state possessing missiles capable of reaching the US.

The Rationale for National Missile Defence

The threat assessment outlined above suggests that appropriate objectives for US national missile defence (NMD) are to protect against small intentional ballistic-missile attacks from countries to which ICBMs might proliferate in the future, and to protect against accidental or unauthorised ballistic-missile launches by any state possessing ICBMs. It is important to note that the US is not defenceless against intentional ballistic-missile threats. First, diplomacy and arms control may halt, or at least delay, the proliferation of long-range ballistic missiles. For example, in exchange for US efforts to begin normalising relations, North Korea has agreed to a moratorium on further ballistic-missile tests. This may have bought time in which to convince Pyongyang that its long-term interests lie in political and economic integration with the rest of the world, rather than in aggressive ballistic-missile development programmes. (Foreign missile sales are one of North Korea's few sources of hard currency.)

Second, if diplomacy fails to prevent the spread of ICBMs, the US has an overwhelming deterrent force, both conventional and nuclear. This makes it unlikely that any emerging ballistic-missile state will threaten, much less attack, the US, except under the most dire circumstances (for example, if the leadership believes it has nothing left to lose by threatening an attack, perhaps to avert unconditional surrender in a war). In general, US deterrent threats are credible because of the interests at stake, the ability to identify the attacker if ballistic missiles are used and the clear capability to deliver an overwhelming retaliatory blow. Negative security assurances notwithstanding, there should be little doubt that the US would respond with devastating force against a state that attacked its territory with NBC weapons.[13]

Finally, if US leaders believe that deterrence might fail, they can authorise conventional pre-emptive counterforce attacks against fixed ICBM sites – although pre-emptive action may appear provocative to other international leaders. Such attacks should be effective against first-generation ICBMs because, typically, these missiles are not mobile, notwithstanding the possibility of deeply buried storage and launch sites.[14] National missile defences thus could insure against the failure of diplomacy to stem the proliferation of long-range ballistic missiles, the failure of deterrence, or ineffective counterforce options. The question is whether the insurance is worth the cost.

The possibility that Russian leaders might lose control over their nuclear-armed missiles, together with the deterioration of Russia's early-warning network, has sparked concern about possible accidental or unauthorised ballistic-missile launches. Since it is difficult for the US to verify that adequate steps have been taken to minimise the likelihood of such attacks, this has become a popular rationale for a national missile defence. Such a defence is under unilateral US control and, by limiting damage, it would reduce the risk of further escalation. However, it is virtually impossible to determine the likelihood of a hypothetical accidental or unauthorised attack. A 1996 Central Intelligence Agency (CIA) report allegedly stated that, although unauthorised Russian attacks are possible, 'under normal circumstances the prospect of an unauthorized nuclear-missile launch or a blackmail attempt using nuclear arms is low, despite continuing turmoil, political uncertainty and disarray in the [Russian] armed forces'.[15] A National Intelligence Council estimate in September 1999 stated that Russian accidental or unauthorised missile launches are 'highly unlikely so long as current technical and procedural safeguards are in place'.[16] Russian political and military leaders also tend to dismiss Western concerns, asserting that their country's missiles are still under reliable control. Similarly, such missile launches by China are deemed to be 'highly unlikely' because its missiles are neither fuelled nor have their warheads mated under normal peacetime conditions.[17]

The probable size of an accidental or unauthorised attack is also difficult to determine. An accidental launch may involve only a few missiles, but the size of an unauthorised attack depends on how far up the chain of command the conspiracy takes place.[18] If Russian field commanders launched ICBMs or submarine-launched ballistic missiles (SLBMs) without authorisation, the attack could comprise up to 200 warheads.[19] If the Russian general staff or commanders of the Strategic Rocket Forces did so, tens or hundreds of missiles could be involved, assuming that subordinate commanders carried out their orders.[20] Inadvertent launches in response to false warning of an incoming attack could involve over 1,000 ICBM and SLBM warheads, depending on the size of the future Russian strategic nuclear force and, more importantly, its alert status.[21]

Consequently, the cost-effectiveness of missile defences against such hypothetical attacks is virtually impossible to determine. Moreover, there are other, cheaper approaches, such as detargeting missiles, reducing their alert rate and fitting them with command-destruct packages, although it is also difficult to assess the cost-effectiveness of these measures, especially since they may introduce other vulnerabilities.[22] Put bluntly, unless one can determine whether accidental or unauthorised attacks are more likely than a catastrophic collision between an asteroid and the earth (which can be estimated with some confidence), it is not clear that more money should be spent on national missile defence than on asteroid defence. These uncertainties do not mean that the problem should be ignored, only that one should not rush to find expensive solutions unless one knows their likely benefit.

The Rationale for Theatre-Missile Defence

Prevailing US threat assessments suggest that appropriate objectives for theatre-missile defence (TMD) are to protect allied cities, thereby making allied leaders less vulnerable to coercion, and safeguarding the basing and over-flight rights upon which a cohesive alliance or coalition depends; and to protect US troops from theatre-range missiles armed with NBC weapons. Protecting allied cities is particularly important because they may be more likely targets for attack than military forces, especially if adversaries believe that their NBC-armed missiles serve as an existential deterrent to prevent complete defeat in a war.[23] Defences are more important for theatre attacks because extended deterrence is less effective than deterrence of attacks against the US; pre-emptive attacks are less likely to succeed given that theatre-range missiles are usually mobile; and passive defences against chemical or biological weapons are typically not available for civilian populations.

Protecting US military forces overseas is, to some extent, an easier mission. Moreover, NBC attacks against military forces may not have a significant impact on US operations unless a large number of weapons are used. Generally, tens of nuclear weapons (fusion bombs, not fission bombs) are required to blunt the type of large-scale operation that the US can mount because a substantial portion of the 25–50 high-priority military targets in a theatre – airfields, ports, command-and-control centres and logistics sites – must be destroyed. Army divisions and ships at sea are difficult to target while they are on the move. Finally, US troops have equipment to protect themselves against chemical and biological weapons. Hence, regional opponents cannot expect to defeat the US outright with small nuclear, biological or chemical arsenals.

An adversary may, however, believe that it can deter the US from intervening in a regional conflict by threatening such attacks. According to Indian Army General K. Sundarji, one of the lessons of the 1991 Gulf War was that states should acquire nuclear weapons before confronting the US.[24] This, however, is debatable. Such threats are not credible because, if important interests are involved, the US will be likely to run considerable risks to avoid the loss of power, prestige or influence that would result if it appeared that it could be deterred by a small country armed with a few nuclear, biological or chemical weapons. If the US were deterred, this would encourage other states to seek similar capabilities, thus providing a powerful stimulus to proliferation. Consequently, although protecting US troops is always desirable, it is not necessarily the most important objective for theatre-missile defence because the likelihood of NBC attacks against US forces may not be high, and defences already exist to some extent.

US Foreign Policy and Ballistic-Missile Defence

US deployment of national and theatre-missile defences could trigger reactions by other states that may in the long term reduce US security. NMD deployments may hinder further reductions in US and Russian strategic nuclear forces. On 14 April 2000, the Russian *Duma* ratified the Strategic Arms Reduction Treaty (START) II, but with the qualifications that Russia could withdraw from START II if: the US failed to abide by it, or if it withdrew from the ABM Treaty; NATO deployed nuclear weapons on the territory of its new members; or the US deployed weapons capable of interfering with Russia's ballistic-missile early-warning system. The ratification document also stated that Russia may consider suspending or withdrawing from START II if a START III is not signed by 31 December 2003. Finally, the instruments of ratification will not be exchanged until the US ratifies the protocol relating to START II and the various ABM Treaty agreements collectively known as the TMD Demarcation Accords (signed on 26 September 1997).[25] Thus, further progress on reducing US and Russian strategic nuclear forces has been tied to restraint on US NMD deployment – although this does not rule out amendments to the ABM Treaty that would allow a limited US defence.

Reductions in Russia's strategic and tactical nuclear forces may not be forthcoming below a certain level regardless of US missile-defence programmes. Russian doctrinal pronouncements suggest that Moscow is placing greater emphasis on nuclear weapons to compensate for relatively weak conventional forces.[26] More importantly, the impending obsolescence of Russia's strategic nuclear force, and the economic constraints on modernising it, suggest that Moscow might conclude a START III treaty, despite concerns about US missile defences, to preserve a semblance of strategic parity. Moreover, making headway on START III depends, in Washington's view, on progress in amending the ABM Treaty to allow an initial US NMD in Alaska (planned for deployment sometime between 2005 and 2007). While there is reason to believe that a compromise on START III and the ABM Treaty might be reached to allow the Alaskan deployment, it is not clear that Russia will make the subsequent amendments required to allow the final planned US NMD architecture, envisaged for deployment between 2010 and 2015. This contains two interceptor sites with a total of approximately 200–250 interceptors and an extensive sensor architecture, including multiple ABM radars and space-based infra-red tracking sensors.[27] If Russia refuses to amend the ABM Treaty, the US has stated that it will consider unilaterally withdrawing from it on six months' notice, as allowed by Article XV. No US ally, much less Russia or China, favours this.

America's NATO allies have traditionally been wary of US proposals for ballistic-missile defence.[28] Among their concerns are that Washington is exaggerating the threat posed by ballistic-missile proliferation; that defences may not work technically; that they may lead the US towards isolationism, rather than involvement in European security; that they may leave Europe as the principal target of attack (although defence coverage could be extended to Europe); that defences are too expensive and may stimulate arms races with Russia or China which could further increase the cost of maintaining security; and that US NMD deployments could lead Russia to deploy comparable defences, which would undermine the independent nuclear deterrent of France and the UK.

The typical European response today, as in the past, is to favour the status quo. However, in the current debate many of these arguments have less force: emerging ballistic-missile states will deploy ballistic missiles that can threaten Europe as well as the US; the evolution of technology suggests that missile defence is more feasible than in the past; the US should be more willing to defend Europe if it can protect its homeland; and it is not axiomatic that an arms race will ensue with Russia and China if the US accommodates their genuine security concerns. Finally, comparable Russian defences may not be forthcoming, largely for economic reasons, thereby ensuring the viability of the French and British deterrent well into the future, while Russian defences should in any case be less threatening to the West now that the Cold War has ended.

China's reaction to US NMD and TMD deployments is of considerable importance, despite the fact that Beijing is not a signatory to the ABM Treaty.[29] Chinese leaders, like many of their Russian counterparts, view US missile-defence programmes as part of a strategy to maintain America's global strategic superiority. China believes that US leaders are exaggerating the threat posed by ballistic-missile proliferation, and that the US is not particularly vulnerable because it can retaliate against any attack with devastating force. The view is widely held in Beijing that Washington will act unilaterally to pursue its interests without regard for the UN Charter, or for Chinese sovereignty. This opinion was reinforced by the US-led NATO bombing in Kosovo in 1999, which took place without UN Security Council authorisation; the accidental bombing of the Chinese Embassy in Belgrade during the Kosovo campaign; and US rhetorical and military support for Taiwan. The revision in September 1997 of the US–Japanese Defence Cooperation Guidelines, which gives Japan greater leeway to support US military operations in the event of a regional conflict, is frequently portrayed as an attempt to contain Beijing, rather than to reassure Tokyo. Finally, leaders in Beijing view anti-Chinese rhetoric in the US as an attempt to portray China as the next enemy. This includes the 1999 Cox Report, which alleged Chinese nuclear spying in the US, the threatened passage of the Taiwan Security Enhancement Act, and US allegations of human-rights violations in China. Thus, Chinese leaders fear, albeit with some exaggeration, that US missile defences are aimed at them, and that the US is emerging as the main threat to China's security.

China's military chiefs are also concerned that a thin US national missile defence will substantially undermine the country's strategic deterrent, potentially removing one means by which China can influence US intervention in a military conflict across the Taiwan Strait. Beijing also fears that US plans will damage the ABM Treaty – a treaty which has ensured the viability of its strategic deterrent for several decades. The treaty's abrogation could derail other international arms-control efforts at a time when China is placing greater emphasis on arms control to help shape the international environment to its liking. China could build a strategic-missile force large enough to overwhelm a thin US NMD system but, given

Beijing's emphasis on economic development, most Chinese leaders currently prefer not to devote large resources to this task.

Whether or not the US should deploy a national missile defence specifically to protect against Chinese ICBMs and SLBMs is, of course, not a question of whether US leaders prefer to remain vulnerable to Beijing out of preference for a strategy based on mutual assured destruction. Rather, it depends on whether the US can achieve an effective defence given the costs associated with the offence–defence arms race that may ensue. Deploying NMD may cause China to increase the size of its strategic-missile force, deploy multiple independently targeted re-entry vehicles (MIRVs), increase research and development for, and seek Russian cooperation on, advanced penetration aids, and consider defence-suppression attacks against vulnerable NMD assets to re-establish an effective deterrent. If the Chinese economy keeps growing at its current rate, the costs to the US of an offence–defence competition could outweigh the benefits of missile defences, especially since offensive forces are typically cheaper than defences.

China's greatest concern is US TMD cooperation with, or deployment to, territories around its periphery. Although designated as 'theatre' missile defences, upper-tier TMD systems can cover the entire territory of US regional allies. This effectively makes them 'national' defences for these countries. The degree of China's concern depends on the country in question. US TMD deployments to South Korea would cause little concern in Beijing, and would probably not upset Sino-US relations because of the clear need to protect the South from attacks by the North, and because China's relations with South Korea are improving. Deployment to Japan poses a long-term problem for China, while US TMD assistance to Taiwan would be viewed as quite provocative. China's concerns should, however, be eased by the fact that the substantial costs of robust TMD defences mean that they may be deployed to its neighbours very slowly, if at all. Regardless of whether TMD systems are sold to South Korea, Japan or Taiwan, US theatre defences could in a crisis be rapidly deployed to territories around China. Consequently, China's concern with US TMD systems is linked to its ability to dissuade the US from regional intervention, especially in defence of Taiwan. Hence, it becomes enmeshed in China's concerns over US NMD deployments.

Japan was only mildly interested in theatre-missile defence until North Korea's *Taepo-dong* 1 overflew its territory in August 1998. Even now, Tokyo has committed only to a single three-year joint project to share the $72 million development cost for the Block II Navy Theater Wide interceptor.[30] Theatre defences may eventually become more appealing to Japanese leaders concerned about the growing threat from North Korea, and the perceived decline in Japanese national power relative to other countries, particularly China. The challenge for Japan is to balance the desire for a more influential role in Asia with the need to maintain a close relationship with the US. TMD programmes are appealing to the extent that deploying theatre systems promotes the closer integration of US and Japanese military forces and strengthens US resolve to defend Japan in a crisis. Ultimately, joint deployment might become part of a renewed security debate in Japan that raises the issue of revising the constitution to allow the use of outer space for military purposes, permit defence spending to increase to over 1% of gross national product, and sanction collective-defence arrangements with other states. But there is also opposition in Japan, both to US and joint programmes, for fear that they will provoke China.

From China's perspective, a more assertive role for Japan, fostered in part by TMD deployments, raises the spectre of Japanese militarism. Chinese leaders specifically oppose Japanese theatre defences because they believe that they will shift the military balance in North-east Asia against Beijing. This claim, while frequently exaggerated, has some merit: Japan's defence budget is roughly equal to China's, its high-technology commercial and military sector is superior and it has capable air defences and naval forces. Japan can, in principle, build ballistic missiles derived from its solid-rocket space-launch-vehicle programme. In addition, Chinese leaders fear that, given the political will to do so, Japan could develop nuclear weapons at short notice. This would give it 'a sword and a shield' if missile defences are also deployed. Finally, TMD cooperation with the US is seen as a vehicle for transferring advanced missile technology in violation of the spirit, though not the letter, of the MTCR, even though Japan already has much of this capability in its space programme. Given China's stake in economic cooperation with both Japan and the US, its opposition to Japanese TMD cooperation may, however, remain rhetorical.

Taiwan is a different matter. Beijing places a 'special emphasis' on Taiwan, and views US military cooperation with Taipei as interference in China's sovereign affairs. US TMD cooperation with Taiwan is embedded in the larger issue of US military sales to the island. Many Chinese leaders thought this matter was settled in 1982, when the US pledged to curb sales in return for a Chinese commitment to seek a peaceful resolution to the Taiwan issue. While the 1979 US Taiwan Relations Act obliges the US president to authorise sales of 'defensive' military hardware to Taiwan, to Chinese leaders this represents blatant interference in their internal affairs. Sales of F-16 fighters, E-2C early-warning aircraft for air defence, three *Patriot* PAC-2 batteries containing 180 missiles for theatre-missile defence and the possible sale of a ballistic-missile early-warning radar test the limits of the 1982 communiqué.

Specifically, theatre-missile defence threatens to interfere with one of the few military instruments China has to intimidate Taiwan. Four unarmed DF-15 missiles were fired towards Taiwan in March 1996 in a bid to influence voters on the eve of the island's national election. The build-up of ballistic missiles in Fujian Province opposite Taiwan may have been intended to affect the outcome of elections in March 2000, but with negative results. China may also regard conventionally armed ballistic missiles as a useful weapon for degrading Taiwan's military capabilities, especially its air force, in war. Beijing does not have the amphibious capability to mount an invasion, or the naval assets to sustain a blockade if the US becomes involved – although aggressive Chinese submarine operations could disrupt merchant traffic with the island.[31] Nor can it launch air attacks without incurring unacceptable losses. Chinese leaders also argue that TMD cooperation is tantamount to a military alliance with Taiwan, which the US eschewed when it normalised relations with the People's Republic in 1979. Although such cooperation hardly equates to the joint political and military decision-making and the capability for joint operations required in an alliance, it would represent greater military integration than hitherto. Ultimately, Chinese leaders fear that improvements in Taiwan's military capability, specifically ballistic-missile defence, will encourage further moves towards independence. This could bring war between China and Taiwan, possibly involving the US.

In short, China's response to US national and theatre-missile defences will depend on the size, type and location of deployments. At the very least, deployment would sour Sino-US relations, and could make China less cooperative on a range of issues of interest to the US, such as the MTCR and non-proliferation treaties dealing with chemical, biological or nuclear weapons. At worst, missile defences could make arms races, and possibly war, more likely. They could stimulate China's nuclear-force modernisation, leading Beijing to withhold ratification of the Comprehensive Test Ban Treaty (CTBT) and to withdraw from negotiations on a fissile material cut-off treaty. China could also become less interested in arms-control agreements that limit the size of its nuclear arsenal.[32] Military cooperation with Russia, especially on BMD countermeasures, could increase since both countries share similar concerns about US missile defences. Consequently, Chinese reactions to US missile defences could reduce US security in the long term.

Deploying ballistic-missile defences may also conflict with US non-proliferation objectives. China's expansion of its nuclear force would, for example, increase pressure on India to do the same, which would in turn make Pakistan follow suit. Nuclear modernisation by any of the five declared nuclear powers in response to another state's missile defences could also undermine the Non-Proliferation Treaty (NPT) by creating the impression that the nuclear powers are not abiding by their Article VI obligations to negotiate in good faith towards the eventual elimination of nuclear weapons. To the extent that NMD or TMD deployments weakened support for the CTBT or for negotiations over a fissile material cut-off treaty, this too could undermine the NPT regime. However, it is difficult to assess how far US missile-defence programmes could in themselves set back Washington's non-proliferation goals. China is modernising its strategic nuclear forces for reasons independent of US missile defences; the CTBT may not enter into force for many reasons, not least the fact that the US has failed to ratify it; and the nuclear competition between China, India and Pakistan is driven largely by regional security concerns and domestic politics. Arguments that US TMD programmes would make it difficult to extend the NPT indefinitely in March 1995 were not borne out. Consequently, although many plausible ripple effects from the deployment of missile defences can be posited, it is difficult to determine which may actually come to pass and, hence, should be the focus of concern for US policy-makers.

The most salient effect of ballistic-missile defences is the risk they pose to strategic stability between the US and Russia or China. This was clearly a concern during the Cold War, and culminated in the ABM Treaty. US President Bill Clinton and his Russian counterpart Boris Yeltsin reaffirmed the importance of maintaining strategic stability when they signed the TMD Demarcation Accords in September 1997, wherein TMD systems are allowed as long as they do not 'pose a realistic threat to the strategic nuclear forces of another Party'.[33] Maintaining strategic stability with respect to smaller powers is less important because upsetting political relations with 'rogue' states is less of an issue; stimulating an arms race with less-developed countries may not be economically disastrous for the US; and emerging ballistic-missile states have little incentive to launch pre-emptive attacks in a crisis because their chances of survival would be low. Maintaining strategic stability is important for the simple reason that substantial nuclear arsenals will continue to exist for the foreseeable future, and there is little evidence that defences can replace deterrence for protecting the US, or any other country, from large nuclear attacks. As long as the major powers rely on nuclear deterrence for their security, maintaining stability between them is important. The question then becomes what level of defence might pose a realistic threat to the strategic nuclear forces of Russia or China.

Performance Criteria
The performance criteria for missile defences can be approached from a political or a military perspective. Politically, defences must be good enough to satisfy an electorate that their leaders have not forsaken their protection, and to convince allied leaders that the US is committed to defending them. This may not require a high level of actual performance. For example, although the *Patriot* system did not intercept many warheads during the 1991 Gulf War, it did allow Israeli leaders to resist public pressure to retaliate against Iraqi missile attacks. Had Israel joined the war, the US-led coalition might have collapsed. From a military perspective, missile defences are useful only if they block enough of the attack to make it tactically or strategically ineffective. In particular, if missile defences are to

protect targets from weapons of mass destruction, they must have very low leakage.

This paper assumes particularly demanding performance criteria: a probability of 0.80 that, in an attack containing up to a few tens of warheads, none gets through a national missile defence; and a probability of 0.50 that no warhead leaks through a theatre defence, even if the entire arsenal is launched at a single target, such as an allied capital. The criterion for national defence is essentially the same as that used by the US Ballistic Missile Defense Organization (BMDO).[34] It covers a limited range of possible Russian and Chinese accidental or unauthorised launch scenarios, as well as small intentional attacks by countries to which ICBMs might proliferate. The criterion for theatre defence appears to be less stringent. However, emerging theatre-ballistic-missile arsenals are larger than intercontinental arsenals, so meeting this criterion is very difficult. If it is met, this would make theatre ballistic missiles tactically useless, and strategically marginal.

Determining the level at which a defence poses a realistic threat to the strategic forces of the major nuclear powers is more complicated because it depends on how many weapons the attacker believes must penetrate the defence for deterrence to remain intact. This in turn depends on the character of the opponent, the interests being threatened and the type of conflict in question. If holding only a handful of targets at risk is deemed sufficient for deterrence, missile defences may not pose much of a threat because a concentrated strike could overwhelm the defence. But if deterrence is believed to depend on holding a wide range of targets at risk, perhaps spread across a defender's entire territory, then even limited defences could seem threatening.

One approach to determining the point at which missile defences might pose a realistic threat would be to use the levels set by the ABM Treaty when it was signed in 1972. The original treaty allowed a maximum intercept potential of 200 warheads (later reduced to 100 by the 1974 ABM Treaty Protocol). This meant a hypothetical ability to intercept around 10% of the 1972 Soviet strategic ballistic-missile force on generated alert (a high combat-alert status, where strategic forces are prepared for war), and between 20% and 30% of its missile warheads on day-to-day alert. However, since tensions between the major nuclear powers today are lower than they were between the US and the Soviet Union in 1972, this criterion seems too restrictive. This analysis assumes that ballistic-missile defences begin to pose a realistic threat if they can block 20% or more of an opponent's ballistic-missile retaliation on generated alert – that is, twice the level allowed by the original ABM Treaty. This is enough to complicate attack planning, foreclose small attack options and raise concerns about the future viability of a ballistic-missile force if defence deployments continue. But it by no means represents the ability to reduce significantly the damage that an attack would cause. Problems with force survival and the reliability of missile systems already reduce the size of a country's retaliatory strike by 20–30% on generated alert relative to that of the deployed nuclear force. Any reduction caused by ballistic-missile defence would be in addition to that which already exists, and to which military planners have already had to adapt.

Countermeasures

The most significant technical advance in ballistic-missile defence over the past two decades has been the advent of hit-to-kill interceptors (interceptors that destroy their target by direct collision, rather than by detonating a high-explosive or nuclear charge nearby). Nearly all of the current US NMD and TMD programmes rely upon such interceptors. By early 2000, only about a third of all US hit-to-kill interceptor tests had succeeded, although the success rate had increased dramatically in the previous year.[35] The most important question is not whether hit-to-kill interceptors will work on the test range – they probably will – but rather whether they will do so if an opponent deploys countermeasures.[36] Countermeasures can be grouped into three categories: those that make target detection and tracking difficult; those that reduce the probability that the interceptor will destroy an incoming warhead (the single-shot probability of kill (SSPK)); and those that simply overwhelm the defence with too many targets.

Examples of countermeasures that make target detection and tracking difficult are 'stealth' techniques that reduce warhead radar and infra-red signatures, large chaff clouds that obscure the trajectory of the missile or warhead, and electronic jamming of ground-based radars.[37] Techniques to reduce exoatmospheric interceptor SSPKs include cooling warheads so that infra-red seekers have difficulty locking onto their targets (cool warheads heat up on re-entry), and encapsulating warheads in large balloons, thereby obscuring their precise location.[38] Manoeuvring warheads and electronic countermeasures that jam radar-homing interceptors can reduce endoatmospheric SSPKs. BMD designers apparently expect exoatmospheric NMD interceptor SSPKs above 0.65, and as high as 0.85 for TMD.[39] While this may not be unrealistic for unitary warheads without countermeasures, it is questionable whether such high values can be achieved under battlefield conditions if countermeasures are present. Countermeasures that saturate the defence include sophisticated decoys that cannot be discriminated from warheads; MIRVs for nuclear-tipped missiles; chemical and biological submunitions; and large attacks that converge on the defence simultaneously, thereby overwhelming its tracking and fire-control capabilities. Booster fragments may appear as exoatmospheric decoys, although advances in radar and optical sensors make it possible to discriminate crude decoys and booster fragments from warheads. Tests with two prototype NMD hit-to-kill interceptors in June 1997 and January 1998 reportedly succeeded in discriminating actual re-entry vehicles from 'decoys, light replicas, and penetration aids' believed to be more complex in design than one would expect from emerging ballistic-missile states.[40] Chemical and biological submunitions are among the most serious potential countermeasures, if they can be designed to withstand re-entry heating, because an adversary could deploy tens or hundreds of submunitions on each ballistic missile, thereby saturating both midcourse and terminal defences. Small submunitions are difficult to track because of their small radar cross-section and, if tracked, are difficult to intercept, due to their size. Finally, lightweight decoys such as chaff and balloons are not effective on missiles with ranges of less than about 350km because these missiles never leave the atmosphere. Hence, these decoys are swept away by atmospheric drag.

Currently, theatre-range ballistic missiles appear to consist solely of unitary warheads. Iraq used no intentional countermeasures during the Gulf War, although the unintentional break-up of missiles and atmospheric manoeuvring made the *Patriot* PAC-2 TMD system largely ineffective. According to open sources, no countermeasures have been reported in missile tests since, although this does not necessarily mean that such tests have not taken place. An interesting question is whether emerging ballistic-missile states are better off flight-testing countermeasures or not. If they do not, they cannot be confident that they will work (which may be acceptable). If they do, the US may learn more about how to defeat the countermeasure than the emerging ballistic-missile state learns about its effectiveness, because such tests must be observed with precision radar and optical sensors. These are instruments that emerging ballistic-missile states typically lack. It is also not clear when decoys or other countermeasures might appear, although it seems reasonable to assume that they will do so, because some are within reach of countries able to produce ballistic missiles.[41] They also may be obtained through foreign assistance.[42] However, the US and the UK took over a decade to develop countermeasures against the relatively unsophisticated radar in the Moscow ABM system.[43] The sensor architectures proposed for US NMD and TMD systems are more robust because they include multiple radar and infra-red sensors, thereby aiding decoy discrimination.

A definitive technical assessment of the effectiveness of these countermeasures and BMD counter-countermeasures is beyond the scope of this paper. Suffice it to say that the effectiveness of BMD systems against simple threats (unitary warheads with only crude penetration aids) may be fairly high.[44] However, the effectiveness of a missile defence against future threats is uncertain, and may be low unless the system can defeat countermeasures of the sort mentioned above. Debates about whether national and theatre-missile defence systems are technically effective will increasingly revolve around the question of countermeasures. This is likely to have little political resonance because of the esoteric physics involved, the fact that future BMD interceptor flight tests will involve countermeasures of some sort, and because debates about whether such tests are realistic cannot be resolved without access to information that will not generally be publicly available. Obviously, it would be exceedingly unwise to field NMD and TMD systems without adequately testing them, under realistic conditions, against a wide range of counter-measures.

Chapter 2

National Missile Defence

National missile defence provides insurance against the failure of diplomacy to stem the proliferation of long-range ballistic missiles, the failure of deterrence, and ineffective conventional counterforce attacks. The question is whether this insurance is worth the cost, given that intentional or accidental attacks are unlikely, other defence needs are more pressing and adverse Russian or Chinese reactions could have long-term consequences for US security. Moreover, while national missile defence is beginning to work on the test range, it has yet to show that it is fully effective against the countermeasures that emerging ballistic-missile states might deploy. Hence, the most prudent approach for the US is to postpone the decision to deploy NMD until the technology matures and the threat becomes more compelling.

However, if threats arise and national missile defence proves technically effective, a thin system with 100 interceptors deployed at one or two sites around the US should be sufficient to protect against attacks containing up to approximately 25 warheads. A defence of this size requires amending the ABM Treaty, but it would not pose a threat to Russia's strategic nuclear force unless this force drops below approximately 1,200 weapons. To avoid posing a threat to China, a US NMD system would have to be limited to between about ten and 25 interceptors, depending on the size of China's future strategic nuclear force.

The Current US National Missile Defence Plan

The current US NMD plan envisages a limited defence consisting of five major components.

- Ground-based interceptors employing exoatmospheric kinetic-kill vehicles (small rockets which use multi-spectral sensors, including long-wave infra-red, to home in on their targets outside the atmosphere).

- Ground-based X-band tracking radars (ABM radars), either collocated with an NMD site or deployed elsewhere.

- Upgraded ballistic-missile early-warning radars to provide warning and cueing information to the X-band radars, and to provide track data on missile trajectories beyond X-band range.[1]

- Two space-based sensor systems: the Space-Based Infra-Red System-High Earth Orbit (SBIRS-High) satellites, which will replace the current Defense Support Program (DSP) satellites for ballistic-missile early warning; and the Space-Based Infra-Red System-Low Earth Orbit (SBIRS-Low) constellation of satellites designed to provide track and decoy-discrimination data on objects in space. In total, six SBIRS-High and 24 SBIRS-Low satellites are to be deployed. SBIRS-Low is designed to observe objects against the cold background of outer space using multi-spectral sensors, including long-wave infra-red. It relies entirely on passive sensors, and will track objects using triangulation.

- A battle-management and command, control and communication system based at the North American Aerospace Defense headquarters at Cheyenne Mountain, Colorado. This will integrate sensor data for early-warning, tracking and decoy discrimination, allocate interceptors against incoming targets, allow human intervention in the launch decision, and provide communication links with the various elements of the NMD system, including a data-link to interceptors in flight.

Three deployment phases were proposed early in 1999. Although current plans differ somewhat, and future ones may do so even more, this proposal provides the best available picture. The initial (so-called 'C1') capability, originally to be operational between 2003 and 2005, is designed to handle small, unsophisticated threats involving approximately five warheads and only simple penetration aids. Originally, it consisted of 20 ground-based interceptors deployed at a single site, either in central Alaska or at Grand Forks, North Dakota, but now the plan is for 20 interceptors to be deployed in central Alaska by 2005, and 100 by 2007.[2] Alaska is the preferred site because it provides better coverage of all 50 US states against potential North Korean attacks. The C1 deployment also calls for a single X-band radar on Shemya Island in the Aleutians; upgrades to all five existing ballistic-missile early-warning radars; the current DSP satellites (or SBIRS-High satellites after around 2005) for ballistic-missile early warning; and three in-flight interceptor-communication systems deployed around the US. (The five existing early-warning radars are located at Clear, Alaska; Beale Air Force Base, California; Cape Cod, Massachusetts; Thule in Greenland; and Fylingdales Moor in the UK.) In the C1 system, DSP (or SBIRS-High) satellites provide a launch-point cue for the upgraded early-warning and X-band radars. Ground-based interceptors typically would be launched after the X-band radar provides an accurate track on an incoming warhead. Decoy discrimination, to the extent that it exists, is provided by the X-band radar and, more importantly, by the optical sensors aboard the kinetic-kill vehicle.

Subsequent deployments are being designed to handle larger threats and more sophisticated penetration aids. Again, the deployment schedule and exact system architecture have not been specified, but the system is most likely to involve a combination of the original second- and third-phase deployments ('C2' and 'C3' respectively) outlined in 1999. The C2 deployment, which was to take place by 2010, consisted of 100 interceptors; three X-band radars collocated with early-warning radars in Alaska, Greenland and the UK; one additional in-flight interceptor-communication system deployed in Missouri; and SBIRS-Low satellites (currently planned for deployment beginning in 2007, with the full system available by 2010). The C3 deployment, which was to occur by 2015, now moved forward to 2011, originally consisted of a total of 250 interceptors at two sites; an additional in-flight interceptor-communication system in Hawaii; a new ballistic-missile early-warning radar and an X-band tracking radar in South Korea; and four additional X-band radars at Beale Air Force Base, Cape Cod and Grand Forks, and in Hawaii.[3] To defend against more advanced penetration aids, the X-band tracking radars provide multiple viewing angles on a target and, more importantly, the multi-spectral sensors aboard SBIRS-Low satellites provide a second type of decoy-discrimination data.

The timetable by which deployment decisions are to be taken is driven by the desire to have an initial NMD system operational by 2005 (which requires construction to begin in Alaska by April 2001), and by electoral politics in the US.[4] In January 1999, $6.6 billion was added to the Defense Department's budget between fiscal years 1999 and 2005 to provide sufficient funding to deploy an initial system if a decision to do so was made in 2000. In October 1999, the deployment date was put back to between 2005 and 2006 in recognition of the high risk associated with the programme's aggressive schedule. The deployment decision was still scheduled for June 2000.[5] However, in March 2000, the third NMD interceptor flight test against a ballistic target missile, which is required before a deployment decision can be made, was postponed until June, thereby effectively delaying the deployment decision until later in the year. Given that further delays are possible, the decision might not be taken until after the new US administration takes office – in the first half of 2001. In terms of electoral politics, outgoing President Clinton may wish to take a decision on deployment before the November 2000 polls so as to remove NMD as an election issue. Calls by some Republican members of Congress for the decision to be delayed until after the election reflect a fear that Clinton may successfully negotiate amendments to the ABM Treaty to allow an initial Alaskan system, while at the same time limiting future NMD options.

Politics aside, it is unclear whether enough information will be available to make an informed deployment decision. Only three test flights against ballistic target missiles will have taken place before the Deployment Readiness Review in July 2000, which was to assess whether sufficient technical progress had been made to warrant an initial decision on NMD deployment. Three flight tests are scheduled each year thereafter until 2005. However, flight tests using the actual production version of the interceptor and kinetic-kill vehicle will not take place until late 2002 or 2003.[6] In addition, flight tests against realistic countermeasures and to verify the lethality of the kill vehicle are scheduled to begin only in 2003, although preliminary tests have taken place.[7] If the decision is made to proceed with deployment, a

Defense Acquisition Board review will recommend procurement of the long-lead-time radars, infra-red satellite systems and command-and-control elements. This will take place in 2001, or perhaps later if the schedule slips. Another Defense Department review, scheduled for 2003, will decide the final production version of the ground-based interceptor, and how many are to be deployed.[8]

In addition to whether the system is technically effective, the criteria on which the deployment decision will be taken are: that a ballistic-missile threat actually exists to the continental United States; whether deployment is allowed by an amended ABM Treaty and, if not, the extent to which US withdrawal from the treaty would damage other arms-control initiatives; and the system's overall cost.

In the wake of the Rumsfeld Commission report, there appears to be bipartisan consensus that the threat to the US is growing. With respect to the ABM Treaty, all current deployment options violate it. While Russia might consider amending the treaty to allow the C1 deployment in Alaska, in exchange for concessions in a START III, it is doubtful that the additional amendments required to make the C2 and C3 options treaty-compliant will be forthcoming because they would open the door to still-more robust US defences by allowing multiple sites and extensive ground-based radars and space-based infra-red surveillance and tracking architectures. Moreover, such amendments would fundamentally alter the ABM Treaty, taking it from an agreement banning nationwide ballistic-missile defences to one that only limits their size, with the possible exception of a ban on space-based weapons. If Russia does not agree to amend the treaty, the US would be faced with the option of unilaterally withdrawing from it.

The research, development and acquisition cost for the 100-interceptor C1 deployment has been estimated at $20.9bn, with a total 20-year life cycle cost (including operating costs) to 2025 of approximately $39bn. The C2 system is estimated to cost $25.6bn (including prior C1 costs), with a total 20-year life cycle cost to 2030 of approximately $54bn. The C3 system with 250 interceptors is expected to have an acquisition cost of $35bn, with a total 20-year life cycle cost to 2031 of about $67bn. These estimates do not include the costs for SBIRS-High or SBIRS-Low because these systems perform other missions besides national missile defence. SBIRS-Low alone is expected to cost an additional $10.6bn.[9]

Technical Requirements for National Missile Defence

The decision on whether to deploy a national missile defence will hinge on whether it is technically and operationally effective. As a political matter, this will be decided by the outcome of the high-profile interceptor flight tests. However, in principle, the decision should be based on whether the system can meet performance levels sufficient to provide useful protection. The effectiveness of a given NMD architecture can be estimated by determining the area of the continental United States that the system can cover, the performance of the surveillance and tracking sensor architecture, and the performance of individual interceptors. Coverage is determined by the location of the NMD site relative to the threat trajectories, the interceptor's flight speed, and its flight time, which depends on the range at which the surveillance and tracking sensors detect and track the missile warhead, and on the speed of the incoming target.[10]

The C1 system provides surveillance and tracking coverage for all hypothetical ICBM trajectories from North Korea to the US. Augmenting this system with upgraded early-warning radars at Cape Cod, Thule and Fylingdales Moor (and the Perimeter Acquisition Tracking Radar at Grand Forks, unless this is dismantled due to concerns about ABM Treaty compliance) would provide a sensor architecture able to track portions of all hypothetical ICBM trajectories from Iran, Iraq, China and Russia. However, interceptors launched from central Alaska will not have sufficient time to reach Russian SLBMs launched from the mid-Atlantic towards targets on the US east coast. Therefore, the C1 architecture provides complete coverage of the US against North Korean, Iranian or Iraqi threats. It also provides complete coverage against Chinese ICBMs. However, the system cannot cover all possible Russian SLBM trajectories. The SBIRS-Low system, multiple X-band tracking radars and the second interceptor site planned for the C2/C3 deployments will provide complete coverage of the US for all ballistic-missile trajectories. Finally, complete coverage is available only with barrage, as opposed to shoot-look-shoot, firing doctrines.[11]

The number of NMD interceptors required to meet a given performance criterion can be derived using a simple model wherein the technical performance of the defence is represented by the probability that the sensor architecture successfully detects, tracks and classifies incoming warheads as warheads (*P(track)*); and the probability that a single interceptor can destroy an incoming warhead (the interceptor single-shot probability of kill (SSPK)).[12] Figure 1 illustrates how the number of interceptors required to defeat a five-warhead attack varies as a function of interceptor SSPK and *P(track)*, for a probability of 0.80 that all five warheads are destroyed. Note that the performance criterion cannot be met, regardless of the interceptor SSPK or how many shots are fired, if *P(track)* is below 0.956. As a practical limit, only four or five interceptors can be launched at each incoming target to avoid saturating the fire-control capability of the defence's battle-management system.[13] The required technical performance for a 20-interceptor defence corresponds to values of SSPK and *P(track)* to the right of the 20-interceptor contour line in Figure 1, assuming that all interceptors can engage the incoming attack.[14] That is, interceptor SSPKs would have to be above approximately 0.60 and detection and tracking probabilities above 0.98 to defeat a five-warhead attack with a probability of 0.80. Figures 2 and 3 (page 36) illustrate the defence performance required to defeat attacks containing ten and 25 warheads respectively, assuming a barrage-firing doctrine and a probability of 0.80 that all the warheads are destroyed. Obviously, as the size of the threat increases, higher detection and tracking probabilities and/or higher interceptor SSPKs are required.

Figure 1 *NMD Interceptors Required for a Five-Warhead Attack*

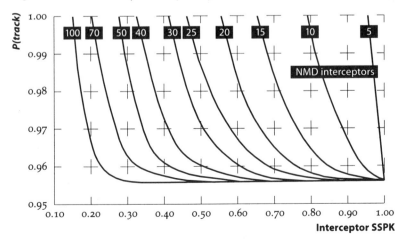

These figures assume that no decoys are present in the attack, or that the defence can discriminate warheads from decoys. Since this may not be possible in all circumstances, the number of apparent warheads with which the defence must contend may be several times the number of real ones. Figures 1–3 can also be used to determine the size of the defence required to defeat an attack

Figure 2 *NMD Interceptors Required for a Ten-Warhead Attack*

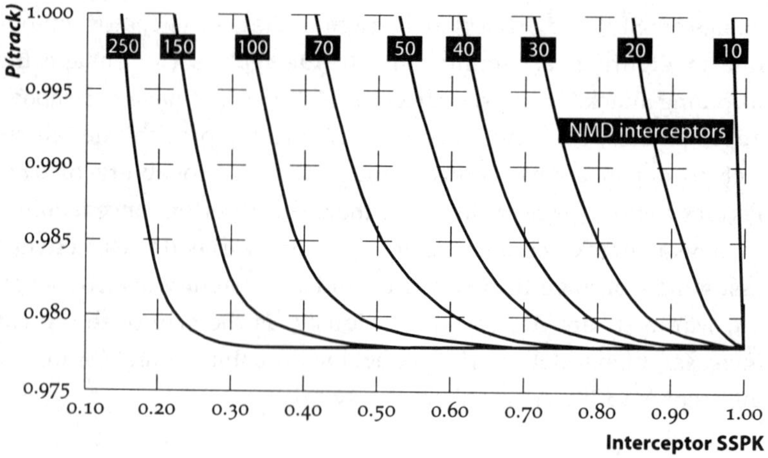

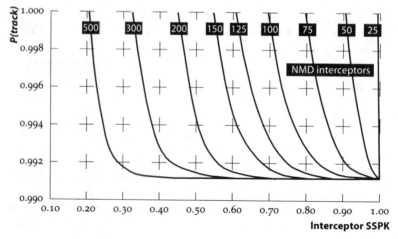

Figure 3 *NMD Interceptors Required for a 25-Warhead Attack*

containing decoys. The fixed attack size in these figures represents the number of real warheads (five, ten or 25). The number of interceptors needed to ensure a probability of 0.80 that all real warheads are destroyed is obtained by multiplying the number of interceptors shown on each contour line by the ratio of the number of apparent warheads divided by the number of real ones.[15] Thus, the number of interceptors required grows linearly with the apparent attack size. For example, if on average two decoys cannot be discriminated from each warhead in a ten-warhead attack, a 100-interceptor defence would have to have interceptor SSPKs and a *P(track)* to the right of a 33-interceptor contour line in Figure 2 if it is to shoot down all ten real warheads from among the 30 apparent ones with a probability of 0.80. As the number of decoys that cannot be discriminated from warheads grows, at some point warheads begin to leak through the defence.

If surveillance and tracking architectures can achieve detection, tracking and warhead-classification probabilities of 0.995 and interceptor SSPKs of 0.75, then a 100-interceptor NMD system that launches four interceptors per target should be able to defeat attacks containing up to 25 warheads. Whether NMD systems can achieve this level of performance is, however, an open question. Proponents clearly believe that this is possible; critics do not. While detection and tracking probabilities between 0.98 and 0.995 and interceptor SSPKs between 0.60 and 0.75 are not heroic performance goals against small attacks containing simple countermeasures, the latter has yet to be achieved on the test range. Nonetheless, one can at least conclude that modifying the ABM Treaty to allow multiple sites, while leaving the interceptor limit at 100, should provide adequate protection against most North Korean, Iranian and Iraqi ICBM threats, assuming that the technical performance described above can be achieved.

Does US National Missile Defence Threaten Russia or China?

The extent to which a thin US national missile defence poses a realistic threat to the strategic retaliatory capability of Russia or China depends on the area each site can defend, the size and character of the attack, and the number and effectiveness of the interceptors.

Russia

A single Alaskan site supported by the C1 sensor architecture should not be particularly threatening to Russia because it cannot cover all possible Russian ballistic-missile trajectories. Moreover, a Russian attack containing more than a few tens of warheads will saturate the NMD radars' track-handling capability. Obviously, if the attack contains more warheads than the number of interceptors deployed, it saturates the defence. The C2/C3 sensor architecture is of greater concern to Russian military planners because it will provide high-quality track data on all Russian missile trajectories heading towards the US, while the addition of SBIRS-Low satellites suggests that the sensor architecture will be less vulnerable to saturation. With the addition of a second interceptor site, the US could, in principle, defend against all possible Russian missile trajectories. Therefore, for C2/C3 deployments the question becomes: how many interceptors pose a realistic threat to Russia's strategic nuclear force?

By 2010–15, Russia's strategic nuclear force under START II or III is likely to contain between 1,150 and 1,800 warheads, assuming the SS-27 (*Topol*-M) ICBM is allowed to carry three MIRVs (see Appendix 2, page 81). Figure 4 illustrates Russia's retaliatory

Figure 4 *Russian Retaliatory Capability against US NMD*

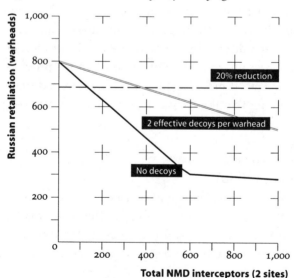

capability (the number of warheads landing on US soil) for a 1,428-warhead Russian force on generated alert as a function of the total number of NMD interceptors deployed at two sites. From the Russian perspective, the interceptors are assumed to be highly effective (an SSPK of 0.9). The size of the Russian force after absorbing a US counterforce first strike (on generated alert) is approximately 800 warheads. Two different attacks are shown: one without decoys and one in which two sophisticated decoys are deployed with each warhead. Russia's retaliatory capability on generated alert levels off at approximately 240 warheads because this is the number of bomber weapons assumed to survive a first strike and penetrate US air defences; hence, they are unaffected by a US NMD system. Finally, it has been assumed that Russia has not withheld any warheads for a secure reserve force. (The number of weapons that Russia might keep back for this purpose is generally believed to be small, and so does not affect the conclusions reached here unless the US can quickly reconstitute its missile defence after the initial attack.)

Using a 1,428-warhead force as an example, it would take an NMD system with approximately 125 interceptors to degrade Russia's ballistic-missile retaliation by 20% – the criterion chosen in Chapter 1 for determining when a defence might begin to appear threatening. This corresponds to a 14% reduction in Russia's overall retaliatory capability when bomber weapons are included. If an average of two effective decoys per warhead are included in the attack, then approximately 375 interceptors would be required to pose a threat to Russia's strategic-missile force. To the extent that Russia can concentrate its retaliatory strike on targets located within the coverage of only one of the two NMD sites, more interceptors would be required to reduce its retaliatory capability by 20%. However, there are limits to how far Russia can adopt such a tactic given the location of its ICBM and SLBM launchers.

Similar calculations can be made for different force structures and for forces on day-to-day alert, as shown in Table 1 (page 40). The smaller strategic nuclear force containing 1,161 warheads represents what might result if Russia's modernisation proceeds at the pace it did during the economic and political turmoil of the 1990s. At the other end of the scale, the 1,794-warhead force is close to the maximum that Russia could deploy under START III. As the table

Table 1 *US NMD and Russian and Chinese Ballistic-Missile Retaliation*

	Number of interceptors causing 20% degradation	
	No decoys	2 decoys/warhead
Russia (generated alert)		
1,794 warheads	190	570
1,428 warheads	125	375
1,161 warheads	90	270
Russia (day-to-day alert)	40	120
China (generated alert)		
102–190 warheads	12–25	36–75

shows, a US system with 100 interceptors should not pose a realistic threat to Russia's strategic nuclear force, except on day-to-day alert, as long as it contains more than approximately 1,200 weapons. If 200 or more NMD interceptors are deployed, as has been suggested for the C2/C3 deployment phases, Russia would have to deploy more than approximately 1,800 strategic nuclear weapons to prevent its ballistic-missile retaliation from being degraded by more than 20%.

The relative vulnerability of Russia's strategic nuclear force on day-to-day alert may be a concern if the US deploys a national missile defence. Russian leaders may come under pressure to bring their forces to higher states of alert early in a crisis so as to improve their ability to saturate the defence. This could have negative consequences because signs that Russia is alerting its forces could lead to misperceptions that exacerbated, rather than stabilised, a crisis, despite the transparency gained through US–Russian military-to-military exchanges in the 1990s. However, the political environment is unlikely to become hostile overnight, thereby giving Russia ample time to increase the peacetime alert rate of its forces in a measured manner. Effective decoys also ameliorate this problem.

Even if a thin US national missile defence does not pose a realistic threat to Russia's strategic-missile force, it could provide the basis for a more robust defence which could do so. Russia would then have to increase the size of its strategic nuclear force in proportion to that of the defence. Retaining extra warheads in the stockpile could act as a hedge against US NMD expansion, allowing Russia to redeploy highly MIRVed ICBMs or SLBMs. Deploying additional strategic delivery systems would, however, only be possible if NMD expansion occurred slowly. If it takes place rapidly, Russia may not have sufficient time to deploy additional systems. In such NMD 'breakout' scenarios, Russia's principal response would be to load more warheads (or penetration aids) on existing strategic missiles. Depending on the size of its nuclear force, Russia will be able to load an additional 270–1,000 warheads. However, NMD breakout is unlikely because an arms race with Russia will be costly, notwithstanding the stronger US economy, since the marginal cost for NMD interceptors (approximately $18m each) is significantly higher than the cost of deploying additional strategic warheads on MIRVed missiles, especially if multiple interceptors must be launched at each warhead.[16]

Finally, NMD breakout is a concern only if the US can gain an exploitable strategic advantage. To do this, the defence would need to block a large portion – 90%, for example – of the opponent's forces.[17] For the above Russian START III forces on generated alert, this would require between 400 and 850 interceptors, even if no decoys are included in the attack and additional warheads are not loaded onto existing missiles. Moreover, Russia would still have a substantial bomber force carrying approximately 500 warheads, requiring an equally effective US national air defence. The time that it would take for the US to reach these defence levels would allow Russia to deploy more ballistic missiles with sufficient throw-weight to carry more warheads; deploy decoys or other penetration aids; or devise ways to suppress the defence. Therefore, although the NMD sensor and command-and-control elements for a more robust defence would be in place with the C2/C3 architectures, it is unlikely that the US could achieve any meaningful strategic advantage by rapidly deploying more interceptors.

China

The C1 sensor architecture for the Alaskan NMD system will be able to detect and track any Chinese ICBMs launched towards the US. Since China currently has only approximately 20 ICBM warheads in its strategic arsenal, this would pose a serious threat to its deterrent against the US. The future size of China's strategic nuclear force is uncertain, and will moreover be affected by the presence of US missile defences. As a rough estimate, China may have between 102 and 190 ballistic-missile warheads capable of reaching the US by 2010–15, but is unlikely to have any long-range bombers which could do so (see Appendix 2, pages 83–85). If this is the case, between 12 and 25 NMD interceptors would reduce the Chinese missile retaliation by 20% (see Table 1). A defence system in Alaska would therefore have to be limited to 20 interceptors (the original C1 deployment size) for it to appear relatively unthreatening to China.

What if Russia Deployed a National Missile Defence?

If the US deploys a national missile defence, Russia might follow suit, notwithstanding its economic problems and statements by Russian leaders that offensive, rather than defensive, responses would be more likely. Table 2 illustrates the size of a hypothetical Russian NMD system that could reduce the strategic nuclear-retaliatory capability of the US, China, France and the UK by 20% after absorbing a Russian counterforce attack on generated alert. Under START III, the US is assumed to deploy 2,500 warheads. By 2015, China is assumed to have approximately 162–290 nuclear weapons capable of reaching Russia (many of them of intermediate range); France 384; and the UK at least 192 (see Appendix 2). France's retaliatory capability includes around 80 bomber weapons, and China's between ten and 30, a portion of which will penetrate Russia's air defences.

Table 2 *Russian NMD and US, French, British and Chinese Ballistic-Missile Retaliation*

	Number of interceptors causing 20% degradation as a function of the percentage of Russian territory attacked			
	100%	50%	25%	25% (2 decoys/ warhead)
US (generated alert)				
2,500 warheads	220	440	880	2,640
France	85	170	340	1,020
UK	40	85	170	510
China (generated alert)				
162–290 warheads	20–36	40–72	80–145	240–435

Four NMD sites are required to cover Russian territory with a barrage-firing doctrine, since it is assumed that Russia will not have the space-based tracking sensors and forward-deployed early-warning radars which would allow larger defended areas. Interceptors have SSPKs of 0.9 from the perspective of US, French, British or Chinese planners. Four attack strategies are illustrated: a retaliatory strike with no decoys against targets located in four, two or one of the four defended areas, and a strike against a single defended area with two sophisticated decoys accompanying each warhead.[18] The last two columns are appropriate for France, the UK and China because their targeting doctrines have traditionally emphasised holding at risk only a few high-priority urban areas.[19] Clearly, a thin Russian national missile defence does not threaten US forces at START III levels, while a defence with 100 interceptors should not pose much of a threat to France or the UK given their targeting doctrines. This is less true for China, because its ballistic-missile force will be smaller and less survivable than that of either France or the UK.

Balancing Costs and Benefits

As an insurance policy against the proliferation of long-range ballistic missiles, national missile defence is probably not worth the costs. First, intentional, accidental or unauthorised attacks by Russia and China are unlikely. Attacks by North Korea, Iran or Iraq are also unlikely because, although these countries may acquire space-launch vehicles or actual ICBMs by 2010 or 2015, deterrence will dissuade them under all but the most dire circumstances, while conventional counterforce strikes can destroy their long-range rockets at fixed sites before they are launched. Second, NMD systems have yet to prove effective on the test range against possible countermeasures. Third, although the total financial cost for the initial 100-interceptor Alaskan system – nearly $40bn – is affordable, the costs of the C2/C3 deployments, at perhaps twice this amount, may not be. Whether affordable or not, these costs mean less funding for other defence programmes. Finally, adverse Russian or Chinese reactions to deployment could undermine US security in the long term. Russian or Chinese nuclear-force modernisation to counter NMD would increase political tensions, and could reduce security cooperation in many areas of importance to the US.

However, if the decision is made to deploy a limited national missile defence, then it behoves the US to proceed slowly. Given that the size and likelihood of a future North Korean, Iranian or Iraqi ICBM threat is uncertain, an initial Alaskan system should contain no more than 20 interceptors to limit the threat such a system would pose to China. This defence could defeat attacks containing up to five warheads, assuming that the sensor architecture obtains detection and tracking probabilities above 0.98 and interceptor SSPKs above 0.60 in the presence of whatever countermeasures might be deployed. If ICBMs appear in North Korea, Iran or Iraq, then the US could expand the Alaskan system to include 100 interceptors – the current C1 deployment plan. This would not threaten Russia, assuming the scenarios Russian planners worry about are ones in which they can increase the alert rate of their forces. However, it would pose a threat to China. A total of 100 interceptors could completely block attacks containing up to 25 warheads or, for example, attacks containing ten real warheads and 20 effective decoys, provided that the sensor architecture obtains detection and tracking probabilities as high as 0.995 and interceptor SSPKs above 0.75 in the presence of likely countermeasures. These interceptors would have to be deployed at multiple sites to handle attacks from all azimuths.

Larger threats would require more interceptors, or better technical performance. A multi-site system containing more than 100 interceptors could threaten Russia's future strategic force if it contains fewer than approximately 1,200 weapons. If the US deploys 250 interceptors at multiple sites Russia will be likely to build up its force to 2,000 weapons or more, unless it is fully confident that penetration aids will be effective. China will find it difficult to cope with such a large defence. However, increasing the size of an NMD system beyond 100 interceptors is not required if the emerging ICBM threat contains fewer than approximately 30 warheads, because the preferred approach is to increase the technical performance of the defence, rather than the number of interceptors.

Chapter 3

Theatre-Missile Defence

Unsurprisingly, most discussions of ballistic-missile defence concern national missile defence, because this is the subject both of the ABM Treaty and of the two prior US missile-defence debates in the late 1960s and mid-1980s. Yet, in terms of programmes, the budgetary emphasis between 1994 and 2000 was on theatre-missile defence, with spending two to three times higher than that on NMD. This is because the problem of ballistic-missile proliferation first and foremost involves short- and medium-range missiles, which can threaten US forces overseas and US allies. Negotiations also focused on clarifying the distinction between theatre and national defence systems in the ABM Treaty, culminating in the 1997 TMD Demarcation Accords.

Despite the resurgence of interest in national missile defence, theatre-missile defence is of considerable importance because the threat exists, extended deterrence is likely to be weaker than homeland deterrence, and US conventional counterforce attacks are less effective against mobile theatre-range missiles. Theatre-missile defence therefore reduces the risks associated with US regional intervention, and reassures US allies. For this reason, some regional powers view US theatre defences with greater alarm than they do US national defences. For example, China is more concerned about US TMD cooperation with Taiwan than it is about NMD deployments in Alaska, although Beijing vociferously opposes these as well. This chapter examines the core US TMD programmes, assesses the technical performance required to achieve meaningful protection and examines the circumstances under which theatre systems might appear threatening to Russia and China.

Current Programmes

Theatre-missile defences can be categorised by the altitude at which they make their intercepts. Systems that intercept targets above altitudes of 80–100km are called exoatmospheric defences. Those that intercept below this altitude are endoatmospheric defences. This distinction is important because, below 80–100km, atmospheric drag strips away lightweight decoys. Between altitudes of 40–80km, atmospheric forces increase, leaving behind all but the most carefully designed decoys, but are still too slight for them to be used by incoming warheads or defence interceptors to manoeuvre. (Lateral rockets are required to manoeuvre the interceptor.) Finally, below 40km aerodynamic forces are appreciable, potentially causing warheads to manoeuvre, thus making them hard to intercept. In the US lexicon, upper-tier TMD systems intercept targets above 40km, while lower-tier systems do so below this altitude. The defended area (the 'footprint') for lower-tier systems is small, while upper-tier systems have larger defended footprints.

The core TMD programmes being funded by the BMDO include the *Patriot Advanced Capability-3* (PAC-3), Navy Area Defense (NAD) and the Medium Extended Air Defense System (MEADS) lower-tier defences; and Theatre High-Altitude Area Defense (THAAD) and Navy Theatre-Wide (NTW) upper-tier defences. PAC-3 is an improved version of the PAC-2 used during the Gulf War, incorporating the new *Erint* hit-to-kill interceptor designed to hit targets up to an altitude of 30km. This gives defended footprints of approximately 40–60km in diameter. The first PAC-3 unit is scheduled to be deployed between 2001 and 2002. The programme currently consists of 1,012 *Erint* missiles, enough to outfit approximately 20 *Patriot* batteries with 48 missiles each. The development and procurement cost is estimated at $10.1bn.[1] However, as with all ballistic-missile defence systems, cost projections and procurement plans change frequently. NAD is based on a modified version of the Standard Missile-2 (the Block IVA) currently used for fleet air defence. In principle, it has defended footprints comparable to those of PAC-3 – although it may be less lethal because it employs a blast-fragmentation warhead instead of a hit-to-kill interceptor. NAD is to be deployed on *Aegis* cruisers and destroyers equipped with vertical launch systems. The programme has been delayed, with the first flight test against a target missile scheduled for 2001, and the initial operational capability expected in 2004. The total planned missile inventory has fallen to 872 from the original estimate of 1,500 (only 407 missiles are currently funded).[2] There is uncertainty over the total programme cost, which was originally estimated at $6.2bn.[3] MEADS, currently an international collaboration between the US, Germany and Italy, is designed to replace the *Hawk* system for defending military forces in the field from air and tactical ballistic-missile attacks.[4] However, due to budgetary pressure in the US, MEADS has been given lower priority, and might be cancelled altogether.

With respect to upper-tier defences, THAAD is designed to engage ballistic-missile warheads at altitudes of between 40km and 150km. It is based on a hit-to-kill interceptor using an infra-red seeker, and has a flyout speed of approximately 2.5km per second. Depending on the incoming missile's speed and the sensor support, THAAD can defend areas several hundred kilometres in diameter.[5] The THAAD ground-based radar is a modern phased-array X-band radar, reputedly with a detection range of up to 500km, which can discriminate simple decoys from warheads, based on their size and radar cross-section. The programme comprises 14 radars and 1,233 missiles, and is projected to cost $17.9bn.[6] Although quality-control problems plagued the early THAAD interceptor flight tests, the two latest tests were successful, and the programme has moved into the engineering and development phase.[7] Of all the core systems, NTW is the least mature. Currently, 650 interceptors are planned for deployment on *Aegis* cruisers and destroyers with vertical launch systems; the total programme cost is unavailable.[8] The Block I interceptor is a Standard Missile-3 (a boosted version of the Block IVA) with a flyout speed of approximately 3km/sec. The Block II interceptor is expected to have a speed of 4–4.5km/sec and, depending on the target missile's speed, the location of the *Aegis* cruiser relative to it and the sensor support, can have defended footprints with diameters of several hundred kilometres to nearly 1,000km. The hit-to-kill payload most frequently associated with NTW is the Lightweight Exo-Atmospheric Projectile (LEAP), which uses long-wave infra-red homing sensors and, reportedly, can only operate above altitudes of approximately 70km.[9]

There is relatively little debate about the need for lower-tier systems to defend high-value targets, although it is questionable whether both PAC-3 and NAD are necessary. Both systems give about the same coverage. PAC-3 is more mature technically and, unlike NAD, can defend inland targets. On the other hand, NAD can be deployed more rapidly to distant theatres, and does not need pre-positioned equipment or personnel in the host nation before war breaks out. Nevertheless, PAC-3's ability to defend inland targets makes it the preferred system. Debates over upper-tier defences are more contentious because these systems have greater potential for intercepting strategic missiles and, hence, for upsetting strategic stability. Again, THAAD and NTW overlap in some respects, although in principle the Block II NTW offers greater coverage because of its higher interceptor speed. It also does not require pre-positioning in a host nation. But NTW has difficulty defending some areas (for example, some states in the Middle East) because of the lack of accessible waters. As of early 2000, the BMDO was planning to deploy THAAD by 2007 or 2008, and NTW by around 2010, if not earlier.[10]

Technical Requirements for Upper-Tier Theatre-Missile Defence

As with national missile defence, the defence performance required for theatre-defence systems to protect against ballistic missiles armed with NBC weapons is ill-defined. The performance criterion assumed here is a probability of 0.50 that no NBC warhead lands on a high-value target. Calculating the defence performance required to meet this goal is complicated by the fact that several TMD layers may exist in the overall defence. For example, some cities and high-value military facilities could be defended by three layers: a boost-phase layer, an upper-tier layer and a lower-tier layer. THAAD and NTW can operate in shoot-look-shoot mode, effectively providing two mid-course layers, albeit with a smaller footprint. PAC-3 and NAD are designed to provide local defence of high-priority targets, such as cities and large military facilities. However, lower-tier defences cannot meet the defence criterion alone because too many interceptors would be needed; other layers must also be present.

The effectiveness of an upper-tier defence depends on the number of sites required to provide adequate coverage of a theatre; the number of interceptors that engage the attack; and their technical performance. The US Department of Defense estimated in May 1999 that, with a barrage-firing doctrine, four THAAD batteries would be needed to cover South Korea, and either four or six to cover Japan, depending on whether additional radars are included.[11] Northern areas of South Korea including Seoul require lower-tier defences because the minimum altitude at which THAAD can intercept (40km) implies that the system cannot defend against North Korean missiles with ranges of under 150km, and hence apogees below 40km. Approximately ten THAAD batteries would be required to cover important areas of the Persian Gulf.

The coverage obtained with the NTW system depends on the location of the ship relative to the missile trajectory, the sensor support and the interceptor flyout speed. NTW would be most effective for defending Japan because it can be stationed between the threat (North Korea) and the territory being defended. In fact, NTW ships stationed in the middle of the Sea of Japan might be able to engage North Korean missiles as they ascend, thereby giving large defended footprints. For example, a single NTW ship should be able to protect almost all of Japan if the Block II interceptor is used, whereas four would be needed with the slower Block I.[12] Defending South Korea requires an additional NTW ship, although interceptors cannot cover the northern two-thirds of South Korea because they cannot defend against missiles with ranges of less than 300km (these missiles have apogees below the minimum NTW intercept altitude of 70km). As noted above, the lack of accessible waters would make NTW less effective in the Middle East.

For the purposes of this analysis, it is assumed that a given theatre is defended with both an upper-tier and a lower-tier TMD system. If PAC-3 is used, the current programme, with around 1,000 interceptors, can provide a lower-tier defence of approximately 20 high-value targets. One or more upper-tier TMD sites are then required to provide an umbrella over the entire theatre.

To assess upper-tier defence requirements, one can either set the technical performance of the lower tier, and then calculate the performance required of the upper, or one can assume that the upper and lower tiers have comparable technical performance, and see how many upper-tier interceptors are required as the performance of both upper and lower tiers is varied simultaneously. This analysis takes the latter approach. Figure 5 illustrates how the number of upper-tier interceptors that must engage a 50-warhead attack to ensure that all warheads are destroyed with a probability of 0.50 varies as a function of the upper- and lower-tier interceptor SSPK and the upper- and lower-tier warhead detection, tracking and identification probability. That is, this plot illustrates the number of THAAD or NTW interceptors that must engage an attack to meet the defence-performance criterion, assuming that high-value targets are defended by an equally capable lower tier.[13] Figures 6 and 7 show similar plots for attacks containing 100 and 200 warheads. The number of PAC-3 interceptors required in the lower tier is not calculated because the current programme is sufficient under almost all conceivable circumstances.

Therefore, assuming that no more than four interceptors are fired at each incoming warhead, the technical performance of the upper and lower tier must lie to the right of the 200-, 400- and 800-interceptor lines in Figures 5, 6 and 7 respectively. That is, TMD interceptors must have SSPKs above approximately 0.50–0.60, and detection and tracking probabilities in excess of 0.94–0.97. (As the

Figure 5 *Upper-tier Interceptors Required for a 50-Warhead Attack*

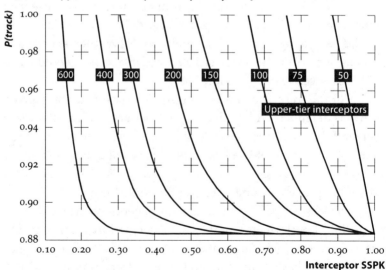

size of the attack increases, so does the minimum value for *P(track)*.)
US planners have stated that the THAAD SSPK should be as high as
0.80–0.85, although there is little test evidence to support this claim.[14]

The assumption that all interceptors can engage an attack is
equivalent to assuming that it is spread uniformly over all defended
areas. However, against a multi-site defence an opponent is likely to

Figure 6 *Upper-tier Interceptors Required for a 100-Warhead Attack*

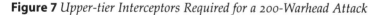

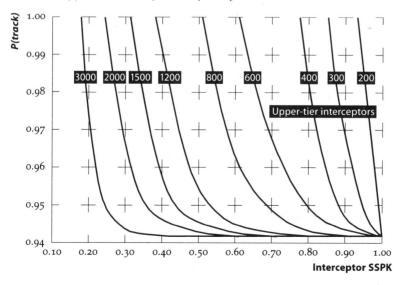

Figure 7 *Upper-tier Interceptors Required for a 200-Warhead Attack*

concentrate the attack to saturate a few defended sites, with the constraint that not all ballistic missiles in the inventory can reach all defended areas due to range limitations, and not all ballistic missiles can be launched in a single day because of insufficient mobile transporter-erector-launchers (TELs). (Fixed launch sites will probably be destroyed rapidly in any war involving the US.) While *Scud*-type mobile TELs can be reloaded in hours, few would be able to launch more than one missile a day because of the need to move and hide immediately after firing, in order to avoid being attacked.[15] Consequently, each defended site must have enough interceptors to handle the maximum number of missiles that can be launched in a single day, assuming that interceptors can be replenished within 24 hours so as to handle subsequent attacks. This maximum attack size is equal to the number of mobile launchers. Historically, countries have tended to deploy between four and 15 ballistic missiles per TEL, suggesting that between 6% and 25% of the arsenal can be launched in a single day.[16] For example, Russia deployed four missiles with each *Scud*-B TEL. Prior to the 1991 Gulf War, Iraq had around 220 *Al-Hussayn* missiles and 14 mobile launchers, giving it about 15 missiles per launcher. Iraq's largest *Scud* attack in a single day in 1991 consisted of 14 missiles, although the average rate was between 4.7 and 1.5 missiles per day.[17]

Therefore, if four THAAD sites are required to protect Japan from attack by *No-dong* and *Taepo-dong* missiles, and if one assumes that North Korea can launch at most 10% of this arsenal in a single day, the total number of interceptors needed to guarantee that no single THAAD site is saturated is 1.3 times the number of interceptors given in Figures 5, 6 and 7.[18] For example, if North Korea has 100 *Scud*-B/ -C and 50 *No-dong/Taepo-dong* missiles in its inventory, 520 THAAD missiles would have to be deployed at four sites in South Korea to ensure that no *Scud* warhead penetrates the upper and lower tiers with a probability of 0.50. Two hundred and sixty THAAD missiles would have to be deployed at four sites in Japan to ensure that no *No-dong/Taepo-dong* warhead penetrates the layered defence, assuming four interceptors are launched at each incoming warhead. Under these circumstances, the technical performance for both upper and lower tiers would have to be to the right of the 400-warhead line in Figure 6 for *Scud* attacks, and to the right of the 200-warhead line in Figure 5 for *No-dong* and *Taepo-dong* attacks. Note that if the Block II NTW system is used as an upper tier to defend Japan, North Korea cannot concentrate the attack to saturate the defence because a single site covers the whole country. Therefore, only 200 NTW interceptors, instead of 260 THAAD interceptors, would need to be deployed. As with national missile defence, if effective decoys are included in the attack, the number of TMD interceptors required to destroy all incoming warheads with a probability of 0.50 is obtained by multiplying the interceptor numbers in Figures 5–7 by the ratio of the number of apparent warheads, divided by the number of real ones in the attack.

Does Upper-Tier Theatre-Missile Defence Threaten Russia or China?

In the Second Agreed Statement to the TMD Demarcation Accords, the US pledged not to deploy theatre defences in number or location so as to pose a realistic threat to Russia's strategic nuclear force. That is, TMD systems would not be used as elements of a US national missile defence, thereby circumventing the ABM Treaty. Under what circumstances and at what levels might theatre defences pose a threat to the strategic forces of a major power? There is relatively little debate that lower-tier systems such as PAC-3 or NAD do not do so. But both Russia and China believe that upper-tier systems might.

Whether upper-tier TMD systems pose a realistic threat to Russia's strategic nuclear force depends on the number of sites needed to cover the US, or a significant portion of US territory, and the number of interceptors that could be deployed at each site. Based on the calculations of the Congressional Budget Office and others, a system like THAAD could, with launch-point cueing from space-based early-warning satellites, defend an area approximately 120km in diameter against a single strategic re-entry vehicle.[19] (An attack involving multiple warheads would reduce the size of the footprint because the radar must share its time between many incoming targets.) About 1,000 120km-diameter footprints would be required to cover the continental United States. Therefore, the current THAAD programme, consisting of about eight batteries, does not pose a realistic threat to any nuclear power with long-range missiles. If the THAAD ground-based radar is cued using track data from early-warning radars or space-based sensors such as SBIRS-Low, but the intercept is still conducted using the THAAD ground-based radar, the hypothetical footprint for a single engagement expands to an ellipse approximately 400km wide by 625km long. About 50 such footprints would be needed to cover the continental United States for northerly attacks, and 80 for attacks from all azimuths, including SLBMs off the east or west coast.[20] Again, the current THAAD programme would not pose a significant threat to other nuclear powers. With accurate cueing, the Block II NTW system cannot defend the interior of the US, despite its higher flyout speed, although it may be able to protect important coastal cities.

Only when upper-tier interceptors are guided in flight beyond the range of their tracking and fire-control radars can THAAD or NTW provide substantial coverage of the US. For example, if accurate track data is obtained early in the trajectory of an inter-continental missile by sensors such as upgraded early-warning radars located outside the US or SBIRS-Low, and this track data is communicated to interceptors in flight, then the hypothetical THAAD footprint against ICBMs increases to a circle about 1,100km in diameter. This implies that 10–12 sites could cover the continental United States.[21] Between three and four NTW footprints would be required under these circumstances. Currently, neither THAAD nor NTW is being designed to accept track data in flight except from their ground- or sea-based radars. However, if SBIRS-Low is deployed, Russian planners fearing the worst might believe that upper-tier TMD interceptors could be guided in flight using its track data, especially if the in-flight interceptor communications system is deployed as part of a future US NMD system. (This assumes that communication receivers are added to TMD interceptors, as they will be to NMD ones.)

Even if upper-tier TMD systems could cover the US, would the defence have sufficient depth to pose a realistic threat to Russian strategic missiles? Figure 8 (page 55) shows Russia's retaliatory capability as a function of the total number of THAAD interceptors deployed at ten sites around the US, for a Russian START III force with 1,428 warheads on generated alert. This plot assumes that Russian planners believe SBIRS-Low or other sensors can be used to guide THAAD interceptors directly. The curves correspond to attacks concentrated against targets in different subsets of the defended areas, so as to saturate the defence. They level off at approximately 240 warheads due to Russia's bomber force. A

Figure 8 *Russian Retaliatory Capability against THAAD*

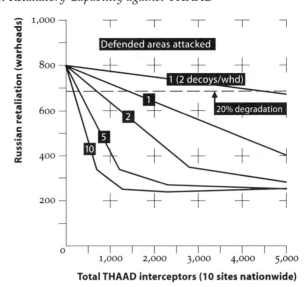

barrage-firing doctrine is assumed for the defence, with an interceptor SSPK of 0.8. This is slightly lower than the SSPK assumed from the Russian perspective for NMD interceptors because TMD interceptors cannot be tested against targets travelling faster than 5km/second. In addition, the attack is uniform, as is the defence coverage, and Russia withholds no warheads for a secure reserve force.

Depending on the number of defended areas attacked, approximately 140, 280, 460, 700 or 1,400 THAAD interceptors deployed at ten sites could make Russian planners believe that 20% of their ballistic-missile retaliation could be blocked. If Russia deployed effective decoys, proportionately more interceptors would be required to pose a threat. The defence would be more effective if Russian forces were on day-to-day alert. But it is implausible that Russia would keep its nuclear forces on a low state of alert if the US deployed TMD systems around its national territory, contrary to assurances that it would not do so. Table 3 (page 56) shows the approximate number of THAAD interceptors that might appear threatening for three Russian force levels and five attack scenarios on generated alert, assuming Russian leaders believe that TMD

Table 3 *THAAD and Russian and Chinese Ballistic-Missile Retaliation*

	Number of interceptors causing 20% degradation as a function of the percentage of US territory targeted				
	100%	50%	30%	20%	10%
Russia (generated alert)					
1,794 warheads	220	430	720	1,080	2,170
1,428 warheads	140	280	460	700	1,400
1,161 warheads	100	200	340	510	1,020
China (generated alert)					
102–190 warheads	13–30	25–60	45–95	70–140	135–280

interceptors can be guided in flight beyond the range of their fire-control radars.

Therefore, if Russian planners fear that the current THAAD programme could provide complete coverage of the US, and that around 1,200 interceptors could be surreptitiously deployed around the country, they would have to alter their nuclear-targeting doctrine to concentrate on targets located in one, or at most two, defended areas to guarantee that less than 20% of their START III missile retaliation is intercepted. This would represent a significant change, and may not be acceptable to Russian leaders. However, Russia's bomber force would still represent a formidable deterrent on generated alert, regardless of the attrition its ICBMs and SLBMs might suffer. Consequently, maintaining a sizeable bomber force should be a Russian priority if the country's leaders are concerned about US missile defences.

If NTW engagements can be conducted beyond the range of the *Aegis* fire-control radar, the number of interceptors that could degrade Russia's strategic-missile force by 20% is calculated in an identical way, assuming an SSPK of 0.8 against strategic warheads. However, a single NTW site can defend approximately 30% of the continental United States. Therefore, the current programme (with 650 interceptors) could appear threatening to Russian planners if their START III force level is much below 1,700 weapons, even if they modify their targeting doctrine to hold at risk targets in only one defended area, the east or west coast for example. Finally, NTW may appear more threatening than THAAD because it can potentially cover the continental United States when stationed at its home port, thereby providing few visible indications that it is being deployed as a national missile defence.

If *both* THAAD and NTW are deployed and a joint command-and-control system can efficiently allocate their interceptors, Russia would have greater cause for concern. For example, if Russia deploys a 1,428-warhead force and relies on a targeting doctrine that holds at risk targets located in one THAAD defended area within one NTW defended area, then 400 THAAD interceptors plus 300 NTW interceptors could appear threatening.

To allay concerns that the US might use TMD systems to defeat Russian strategic (or theatre) missiles, the US and Russia agreed as part of the TMD Demarcation Accords that theatre systems 'will not be deployed by the Parties for use against each other', and that 'the scale of deployment – in number and geographic scope' would be consistent with the threats confronting each country.[22] Confidence-building measures also provide for annual data exchanges on each side's programmes; for the identification of test ranges; and for ten days' notice of tests. To reduce concerns further, the US should consider allowing on-site inspections at garrisons and at facilities producing TMD missiles, launchers and radars, so as to reassure Russia that it is not about to expand its capabilities rapidly.

Table 3 also shows the size of US THAAD deployments that could appear threatening to China's strategic nuclear force. A relatively small upper-tier TMD system could do so. Of course, China is more concerned about US upper-tier TMD systems being deployed in, or sold to, territories around its periphery, especially Taiwan.

What if Russia deployed advanced upper-tier TMD systems? It is unlikely to do so by 2010. However, if it did, these defences would be less effective than US systems against strategic missiles because they would be supported by a less capable missile-detection and tracking sensor architecture. It is unlikely that Russia will deploy satellites comparable to SBIRS-Low, and the country has no early-warning radars located outside of the territory of the former Soviet Union. For example, it would take between 50 and 100 'THAAD-like' footprints to cover Russia's populated regions. Such a system deployed around Russia's national territory should not appear threatening to three of the four major nuclear powers until more than 500 interceptors are deployed, assuming that the US, France and the UK concentrate their retaliatory strikes, to varying degrees, so as to saturate the defence. China could feel threatened unless it concentrates its retaliatory strike against only a few defended areas.

Consequently, current US TMD programmes should provide broad protection against emerging theatre-range ballistic-missile threats, assuming these systems work technically. But fiscal constraints will probably limit these programmes to fewer interceptors than currently planned. In terms of Russian and Chinese perceptions, this might not be an entirely bad thing because the current large THAAD and NTW programmes might appear to threaten Russian and Chinese strategic missiles. To minimise this threat, confidence-building measures would be required to show that TMD systems cannot conduct engagements beyond the range of their fire-control radar. Limiting the total number of deployed upper-tier interceptors to between 600 and 800 would also help. An upper-tier defence with 800 interceptors, when combined with an equally capable lower tier, should be able to block theatre-missile attacks containing up to 200 warheads, assuming that both upper and lower tiers can achieve interceptor SSPKs above 0.6, and detection and tracking probabilities above 0.97. These are not unrealistic goals against relatively simple threats, although such interceptor performance has yet to be demonstrated on the test range, especially in the presence of countermeasures.

Chapter 4

Boost-Phase Ballistic-Missile Defence

Ideally, the US should want a ballistic-missile defence that is effective against emerging threats, whether of short, intermediate or intercontinental range, and which is effective against counter-measures – yet poses relatively little threat to the strategic missiles of Russia or China. Such a defence may exist, in the form of airborne boost-phase interceptors. However, this defence cannot protect against Russian or Chinese accidental or unauthorised missile launches – potentially the system's greatest drawback.

Boost-phase ballistic-missile defence is attractive because rocket boosters are easy to detect and track; they are more vulnerable and, hence, easier to destroy than warheads; determining that the defence has destroyed a booster is easier than it is for a warhead; and the entire payload (warheads and penetration aids) can be destroyed in a single shot. Moreover, if intercepted several seconds before the booster burns out, the debris will fall short of the target area, potentially avoiding collateral damage to friendly territory. Boost-phase defence also only needs to cover the opponent's territory, as opposed to all friendly territory within range of its ballistic missiles. Intelligence information may be used to further pinpoint possible launch areas.[1] Finally, countermeasures against boost-phase defence, such as fast-burn boosters and booster decoys, are difficult to build.

These advantages animated President Reagan's Strategic Defense Initiative. However, unlike boost-phase strategic defence against Russia, against most emerging ballistic-missile states it does not require space-based weapons. Instead, airborne platforms can be used. This is an important difference because, while airborne boost-phase systems may be effective against theatre- and intercontinental-range missiles launched from small states such as North Korea, they are not effective against ICBMs launched from large countries such as Russia and China, or against any country that can deploy SLBMs. Consequently, airborne boost-phase defences pose relatively little threat to the strategic forces of any of the five major nuclear powers.

Naval boost-phase interceptors have also been proposed for national missile defence.[2] They have some advantages over airborne interceptors, such as the fact that naval platforms have greater endurance, and naval interceptors can be larger and, hence, faster. However, they are generally less effective for theatre-missile defence because they cannot get close enough to theatre-range missiles in their boost phase, although they may be able to hit them in their ascent phase after booster burnout. Even for national missile defence, naval platforms may lack accessible waters, and they may pose a threat to Russian and Chinese SLBMs. Similarly, Russian naval boost-phase interceptors might appear to threaten US, French or British SLBMs. This chapter focuses on airborne boost-phase defences because, with some notable operational limitations, they are attractive for TMD, and may also be an effective national defence against emerging ICBM threats.

Airborne Systems

There are several advanced technology-demonstration programmes for intercepting theatre-range ballistic missiles in their boost phase. These are based on a high-speed airborne interceptor (ABI) launched from fighter aircraft or unmanned aerial vehicles (UAVs); a high-power airborne laser (ABL) carried aboard a Boeing 747-400F; or a space-based laser. Space-based lasers are banned for national missile defence by the ABM Treaty, and for theatre-missile defence by the Second Agreed Statement in the TMD Demarcation Accords. Nevertheless, they remain of interest to the US Air Force and some members of Congress, and $139m has been allocated for a 'space-based laser integrated flight experiment', a series of ABM Treaty-compliant ground, airborne and space-based experiments designed to demonstrate technical feasibility. A non-ABM Treaty-compliant test is planned for around 2012.[3]

The Airborne Interceptor

The airborne-interceptor concept is based on a high-speed rocket employing a small kinetic-kill vehicle for a payload, which homes in on the booster's infra-red signature. Interceptors could receive booster track information from an airborne radar and/or from an infra-red sensor, although it could conceivably come from space-based sensors, or from sensors aboard the launch platform itself. Airborne sensor platforms should be able to provide adequate detection and tracking from approximately 500km away. The original ABI concept was proposed for theatre-missile defence, and used fighter aircraft as a launch platform. Attention then shifted to UAVs, starting in the early 1990s with the *Raptor/Talon* programme. After the cancellation of this programme, preliminary studies analysed the effectiveness of the US Air Force *Global Hawk* UAV as a launch platform. The *Global Hawk* is attractive because it has a larger payload of 1,000kg, a higher operating ceiling and longer endurance.[4] The only currently active airborne-interceptor programme is a small joint US–Israeli effort, which uses a 1.4km/sec interceptor called *Moab* carried aboard an Israeli UAV.[5]

The lethal range of an airborne interceptor depends on its flyout speed, the missile booster's burn time and the length of time between the launch of the missile and that of the interceptor. A two-stage ABI based on current rocket-motor technology, with a mass of approximately 600kg, can achieve maximum speeds of around 5.1 km/sec with a 35kg kinetic-kill vehicle as its payload. Boost times for theatre-range ballistic missiles are typically between 70 and 150 seconds, depending on their range and design, whereas those for ICBMs are around 200 seconds for solid-fuel missiles, and 250–300 seconds for liquid-fuel ones. The delay between missile and interceptor launch stems from the time it takes to establish an accurate track and positively identify the target as a threatening missile: typically between 20 and 45 seconds. Using 45-second launch delays as a conservative estimate, a 5.1km/sec two-stage ABI would have intercept ranges of approximately 50–200km for short- and medium-range missiles; 400km to 600km for intermediate-range missiles; and 800km to 1,000km for liquid-fuel ICBMs.

Figure 9 (page 62) illustrates the coverage of North Korea with a 5.1km/sec ABI and a 45-second launch delay against *Scud*-B, *Scud*-C, *No-dong* and *Taepo-dong* 1 missiles. It also shows coverage against

Figure 9 *ABI Coverage of North Korea*

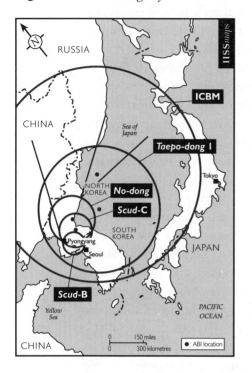

a hypothetical North Korean ICBM based on a three-stage *Taepo-dong* 2, along with the ground-trace for ICBMs launched from two locations towards the US east coast, west coast and Hawaii. The boost times associated with these missiles are 70, 85, 93, 165 and 243 seconds respectively. The intercept ranges for the *Scud*-B, *Scud*-C, *No-dong* and *Taepo-dong* 1 (assuming that intercept occurs four seconds before booster burnout) are 70km, 135km, 170km and 480km respectively. The ABI intercept range against a hypothetical North Korean ICBM is approximately 850km, assuming an intercept at six seconds before burnout. The circles in the figure represent the ABI engagement zones – the range out to which a 5.1km/sec ABI can intercept a missile of a given type several seconds before booster burnout. Four to six ABI zones would be required to cover all possible North Korean *Scud*-B launch locations; two to three would be needed for *Scud*-C launches; two for *No-dongs*; and only one to defend against intermediate- or intercontinental-range missiles. For the latter, the ABI launch platforms could be located over international waters in the Sea of Japan. Fewer ABI zones would be required if potential launch areas could be pinpointed from intelligence information. Therefore, a relatively small number of ABI engagement zones is sufficient to provide coverage against North Korean theatre-range missile threats, and a single location over the Sea of Japan is enough for a boost-phase defence against North Korean ICBMs launched towards the US. Four to six zones would also provide reasonable coverage of Iraq, although this would be insufficient for a large state such as Iran unless ABI reaction times could be reduced below 45 seconds, and ballistic-missile launch areas could be pinpointed.

The number of interceptors required to meet a given performance criterion can be determined from calculations similar to those for upper-tier defences, except that airborne systems do not have enough time to operate in shoot-look-shoot mode. Figures 5, 6 and 7 (pages 50–51) can be used to determine the number of ABIs that must engage an attack to guarantee a probability of 0.5 that no warhead gets through a defence consisting of a boost-phase layer and a second layer comprising either an upper- or a lower-tier defence. Here, the detection and tracking probability and interceptor SSPK associated with the boost-phase layer pertains to tracking and intercepting the missile booster; the technical parameters associated with the subsequent upper- or lower-tier layer relate to tracking and intercepting the warhead.

The number of interceptors that must be on station in any given zone is derived from the number that must be launched at each missile to meet the performance criterion, multiplied by the maximum number of missiles that can be launched from within the ABI lethal range in the time that it takes to replace platforms that have exhausted their interceptors (several hours). This is assumed to be the same as the maximum daily launch-rate discussed in Chapter 3 for upper-tier TMD systems, assuming as a worst case that all mobile TELs for short- and medium-range missiles can be concentrated within a single ABI engagement zone, and that these missiles can all be launched within a few hours. (Concentrating mobile launchers in this way makes them more vulnerable to air attack; moreover, if their movement is detected in time, ABI launch platforms can be concentrated against them.) The required number of launch platforms equals the number of interceptors divided by the carrying capacity of each platform (four to eight ABIs for fighter aircraft, and approximately two for large UAVs). Since fighters can maintain combat air patrols for about eight hours, three are required to provide 24-hour coverage, with another one or two aircraft spare in case major maintenance problems arise. With a nominal on-station time of 24 hours, two *Global Hawk* UAVs would be required to maintain one in the air for 24 hours. For example, a total of 200 UAVs and 800 ABIs with an SSPK above 0.60 and a tracking probability above 0.97 could cover five zones and guarantee, with a probability of 0.50, that no warheads would penetrate a two-layer defence for attacks containing up to 200 unitary warheads, assuming a maximum salvo-launch capability of ten missiles within a few hours and no decoys. In terms of expenditure, 200 *Global Hawks*, 800 ABI missiles and eight airborne radar aircraft would cost roughly $8bn. If new fighter aircraft are bought as the launch platforms, the acquisition cost would increase by about $5bn.

Boost-phase BMD is the only active defence capable of handling countermeasures such as chemical and biological sub-munitions, as well as other sophisticated penetration aids that may defeat upper- or lower-tier TMD systems. The number of ABIs required, when acting alone, to ensure a probability of 0.50 that no missile gets through a single boost-phase layer is shown in Figure 10, as a function of the interceptor's SSPK and a missile detection and tracking probability of 0.98. Thus, a single ABI boost-phase layer may be able to block 20–30 missiles by itself, assuming that four to five interceptors are fired at each target, and that the SSPK is around 0.6–0.7. In larger attacks, some missiles will get through, thereby presenting subsequent layers of the defence with a large number of chemical and biological submunitions. Thus, a boost-phase national defence based on the airborne interceptor could completely block 20–30 North Korean ICBMs, even if they carried fractionated chemical and biological submunitions, assuming that 100–150 interceptors can engage these missiles over whatever time window they can be launched.

Figure 10 *ABIs Required to Defeat Fractionated CBW Payloads*

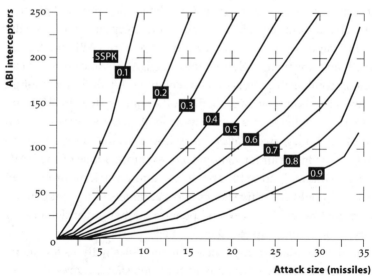

There are several operational limitations to the ABI system that make it a less than perfect defence. First, the launch platforms and, for large states, perhaps also the airborne sensor platforms, cannot provide adequate coverage against short- and medium-range ballistic missiles from orbits outside the opponent's airspace. Launch platforms would of course enter enemy airspace within the first few minutes of a conflict. However, the threat of a ballistic-missile attack may exert considerable political leverage before war actually breaks out. Violating a country's airspace with an armed aircraft is itself an act of war. Second, ABI platforms may not survive enemy air defences. While many small states have relatively weak air defences, and placing interceptors on UAVs flying above 60,000 feet minimises the risk of them being shot down, advanced defences like the Russian SA-10 and SA-12 surface-to-air missiles could pose problems should they be exported to emerging ballistic-missile states. Making the ABI launch platforms stealthy may solve the problem, but this would make the UAV considerably more expensive. After a war starts, the air defences of small states can be suppressed. If the use of NBC-armed ballistic missiles is threatened to forestall the defeat of the regime, then this is likely to happen towards the end of a conflict. In this case, ample time should be available to establish air superiority over countries like North Korea, Iraq or Iran. Third, keeping airborne platforms on station for months on end would be very costly (although it has been done). Fourth, there are unresolved technical challenges associated with the command and control of UAVs loitering over enemy airspace, and with retrieving UAVs carrying live munitions. Finally, political issues need to be thought through regarding when such defences can be forward deployed, and whether this might appear to an opponent to be escalatory.

The Airborne Laser

The US Air Force has selected the airborne laser as its preferred boost-phase TMD programme, and has devoted $1.6bn to developing a prototype to be tested between 2003 and 2005. The ABL concept is based on a three-megawatt oxygen–iodine laser carried aboard a Boeing 747-400F. The current programme envisions deploying seven aircraft, with the first operational version available sometime between 2007 and 2014, depending on funding. This number of aircraft could support two orbits 24 hours a day. While enthusiasts are confident that the underlying technology is sound, several key hurdles must be cleared before the airborne laser can be declared technically feasible. These include scaling the power up from small lasers to reach 3MW, while at the same time keeping the unit's overall weight down so that the aircraft can fly at high altitudes, avoiding as much atmospheric turbulence as possible; a demonstration that adaptive optics can compensate for the atmospheric turbulence that the laser beam is expected to encounter; and high-precision optical pointing and tracking systems that can work on board a 747 given the vibration of the aircraft. The novel character of this weapon means that the challenges will be greater than those posed by other missile-defence programmes.

Lasers destroy boosters by depositing sufficient energy to weaken the booster's casing. This either punches a hole in it, causing it to vent rapidly, or makes it collapse under the load from the missile's acceleration. The time that this takes depends on the booster casing's material, the range from the laser to the target, the power of the laser and the diameter of the optics. Since the laser dwells on each booster until it is destroyed, its effectiveness cannot be modelled by a simple SSPK independent of range. In theory, the SSPK should be close to unity if the target is within the laser's lethal range, and nearly zero if it is beyond it.

One analysis concludes that the airborne laser's maximum lethal range should be about 320km against *Scud*-B and *No-dong* missiles, and about 470km against the *Scud*-C or *Al-Hussayn*.[6] Therefore, a single ABL stationed 90km outside of North Korean airspace covers almost the entire country, though two or more locations would be required to cover all of Iraq. For large countries such as Iran, the airborne laser cannot cover all possible launch locations from orbits outside of the opponent's airspace, implying that the ABL would have to penetrate enemy airspace – a very risky tactic with such a large, high-value aircraft. If the laser must contend with several missiles at once, the maximum lethal range is reduced because it must split its time between the targets. Seven aircraft supporting two orbits should provide an adequate initial boost-phase theatre-missile defence. However, this assessment could change dramatically if the lethal ranges for the laser cited here drop by more than 20% due to countermeasures such as hardening the booster against laser radiation, rotating it in flight to spread the laser energy, or using salvo launches. Although the estimated programme cost ($5bn for the acquisition of seven aircraft, with a total life cycle cost over 20 years of $11bn) makes this the cheapest boost-phase option, the potential vulnerability of the ABL to several straight-forward countermeasures means that it is less attractive than the airborne interceptor.[7] Moreover, the ABI lethal range increases more rapidly than that of the ABL for missiles with longer boost times, implying that the ABI is more effective against emerging ICBM threats. The maximum range of the ABL against strategic missiles has been estimated at between 300km and 400km.[8]

Does Airborne Boost-Phase Defence Threaten Russia or China?

If airborne boost-phase systems, especially the ABI, are effective against theatre- and intercontinental-range ballistic missiles launched from emerging ballistic-missile states, might they also be effective against Russian or Chinese ICBMs or SLBMs? In fact, airborne systems do not pose a realistic threat to Russian or Chinese strategic ballistic missiles.

Figure 11 (page 68) illustrates the ABI coverage of potential Russian ICBM and SLBM launch locations, and of potential Chinese ICBM launch locations, together with the boost-phase ground-trace for ICBMs and SLBMs launched from representative sites towards targets on the US east and west coasts. The lethal range for a 5.1km/sec ABI against Russian SS-25/SS-27 (*Topol*-M) solid-fuel ICBMs is estimated at approximately 600km; that against Russian liquid-fuel SLBMs such as the SS-N-23 at approximately 800km (although the future SS-NX-28 is supposed to be a solid-fuel SLBM); and the estimated lethal range against Chinese DF-5A liquid-fuel ICBMs is approximately 850km (although future Chinese ICBMs will have solid fuel and, presumably, shorter boost times). These estimates are optimistic in that they ignore possible constraints imposed by the range of the detection and tracking sensors, which may reduce the lethal range unless space-based sensors such as SBIRS-High can be used to guide airborne interceptors to their targets.

As Figure 11 shows, it takes between six and seven ABI engagement zones to cover Russia's ballistic-missile submarine (SSBN) bastions near its territory. If in the future Russia's SLBM force is located entirely with the Northern Fleet, this figure drops to

Figure 11 *ABI Coverage of Russian and Chinese Strategic-Missile Sites*

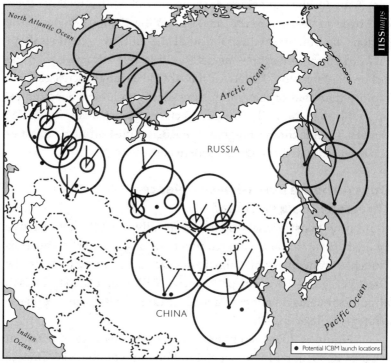

around three. Despite a preference for basing submarines in bastions, Russian SSBNs could deploy to the open ocean. In this case, approximately 20 ABI zones would be required to cover all possible SLBM launch locations in the North Atlantic, and 30 for all possible launch locations in the North Pacific. If Russia deploys single-warhead ICBMs in former SS-18 and SS-19 silos under START II, and up to 350 mobile *Topol*-Ms at ten garrisons, at least six additional ABI zones would be needed to cover all possible ICBM launch locations.[9] In Figure 11, the smaller circles with a radius of 150km represent the area into which mobile ICBMs could deploy within ten hours after leaving their garrison. Larger deployment areas may be possible, but logistics constraints eventually limit their size.

The US would have to keep ABI launch platforms aloft continuously in at least nine zones to cover future Russian ICBM and SLBM launch locations, and potentially three to four times this number if Russia sends its SSBNs into the open ocean. This would be a daunting task. Aircraft and UAVs may not, for example, have enough fuel to reach these locations from distant allied airfields. More importantly, ABI launch platforms, the ABL, any sensor aircraft and their tanker support would all be vulnerable to Russian air defences. While it is plausible to think of suppressing the air defences of a weak state, Russia's are an entirely different matter. In addition, the airfields from which ABI or ABL operations originate would be vulnerable to Russian attack because they are few in number and relatively easy to identify. (Emerging ballistic-missile states would have difficulty carrying out such attacks.) Finally, Russian salvo launches would make any residual airborne boost-phase system even less effective. Hence, an ABI (or ABL) boost-phase defence would pose very little threat to Russian ICBMs and SLBMs. This is largely for operational reasons, not because the ABI could not intercept a Russian strategic missile if it were within range.

Airborne boost-phase systems may pose more of a threat to Chinese strategic missiles because China has fewer ICBM launch sites, the boost times for Chinese ICBMs may be longer than for Russian ICBMs, and Chinese SLBMs may not be effective due to US anti-submarine operations. Still, ABI or ABL platforms would have to penetrate Chinese airspace to cover all possible ICBM launch locations, thereby exposing themselves to Chinese air defences. Hence, the threat posed to China's strategic missiles by airborne boost-phase systems should be manageable. However, the threat posed by ABI or ABL systems to Chinese theatre-range missiles would be of concern to Chinese leaders, especially if they were used to defend Taiwan from DF-15 missiles fired across the Taiwan Strait. If Russia ever develops airborne boost-phase systems, they would not pose a threat to US, French, British or Chinese strategic forces.

Therefore, airborne boost-phase ballistic-missile defences, in particular the airborne interceptor, offer the prospect of highly effective, robust theatre *and* national defences against emerging ballistic-missile states – yet they pose very little threat to the strategic nuclear forces of the five major nuclear powers. Naval boost-phase interceptors for national missile defence also may be attractive, but are less effective against theatre-range missiles and could appear threatening to any state that relies on submarines for its strategic deterrent. The principal drawback with these systems is that they offer no protection against accidental or unauthorised Russian or

Chinese launches. Moreover, there are technical and operational limitations that need to be examined in greater detail before the US could commit to these defences. Nevertheless, given that a land-based NMD system could appear threatening to Russia, and certainly would to China, it behoves the US to examine boost-phase alternatives more closely before proceeding far with the current NMD plan.

Conclusion

The threat posed by the proliferation of ballistic missiles is real and growing. However, the US is not defenceless. Diplomacy and arms control may forestall these threats, deterrence should prevent attacks in all but extreme circumstances, while conventional counterforce strikes may destroy the opponent's missiles, at least those at fixed sites, before they are launched. Assuming that they work, NMD and TMD systems could provide insurance against the failure of these measures, or against a small accidental or unauthorised ballistic-missile launch. The question is whether this insurance is worth the cost, both in money spent, and in possible negative international reactions. While some reactions can be dismissed as rhetoric, it would be a serious mistake for US leaders to press on without taking into account other states' genuine security concerns.

On balance, there is no immediate need to deploy a national missile defence because accidental and unauthorised Russian or Chinese attacks are unlikely and, although developing states may deploy rudimentary ICBMs by 2010 or 2015, deterrence and conventional counterforce options should keep the risk acceptably low. Moreover, ground-based NMD systems have yet to prove themselves effective in tests against plausible countermeasures. The 20-year life cycle cost for the initial Alaskan system is estimated at $39bn, which may be affordable, but subsequent larger deployments, which cost twice this amount, may not be. Spending money on missile defence means less funding for other programmes. Finally, adverse Russian or Chinese reactions could undermine US security in the long term. The US should therefore postpone its decision on deploying NMD, at least until the technology matures and there has been more time to evaluate the potential deletrious impact that deployment could have on other US security interests.

If the decision is made to proceed with deployment, it should happen slowly. Given that the size of the future ICBM threat is uncertain, the initial Alaskan system should be limited to 20 interceptors, thereby minimising the impact on China's future strategic nuclear force. Assuming it works, a defence of this size could protect the US from attacks containing up to five warheads. If ICBMs actually appear in North Korea, Iran or Iraq, the Alaskan system could be expanded to include 100 interceptors within several years. This would not be particularly threatening to Russia, though it would be to China. A hundred interceptors could completely block attacks containing up to 25 warheads or, for example, ten real warheads and 20 effective decoys, provided the sensor architecture obtains detection and tracking probabilities as high as 0.995 and interceptor SSPKs above 0.75.

A multi-site NMD containing more than 100 interceptors could threaten Russia's future strategic-deterrent force if it contained fewer than 1,200 weapons. It should thus be avoided unless the threat becomes unambiguously clear. Unless it was very confident that its countermeasures would be effective, Russia would probably respond by increasing its strategic force to 2,000 weapons or more. Russia's strategic bomber force will become more important in a world with limited US NMD, because it circumvents missile defences. China, on the other hand, would find it difficult to build a strategic force large enough to overwhelm such a defence. Moscow is unlikely to deploy a comparable NMD system. Even if it did so, more than 100 interceptors would be required to threaten the US, French, British or Chinese strategic nuclear deterrent.

If a limited US defence exists, NMD 'breakout' should not be much of a concern. Despite the fact that the infrastructure for a more robust defence would be in place, the US would have to deploy many hundreds of interceptors to gain any coercive leverage over Russia at START II or START III force levels. Russia can respond by loading more warheads on missiles previously downloaded under START II, and by stepping up the production of new missiles, at a fraction of the cost of expanding the defence.

Any decision to deploy a limited NMD system will require modifying the ABM Treaty. Russia may be amenable to amendments that allow an initial Alaskan deployment, if it receives concessions in parallel START III negotiations. There is, however, little evidence that such a compromise is possible. Changes that allow more robust NMD architectures, as envisaged in the US C2/C3 deployments, will be much more difficult to negotiate. However, a 100-interceptor system, perhaps based at multiple sites, should not interfere with further US–Russian strategic arms control until levels of around 1,200 weapons are reached. In any case, the preferred US approach should be to try to amend the treaty, rather than withdraw from it.

The proliferation of theatre-range ballistic missiles poses the greatest threat in the short term. The most challenging objective for theatre defence is to protect allied cities from regional opponents with NBC-armed ballistic missiles. Layered defences are attractive because they offer the prospect of low leakage. Current US TMD programmes should provide broad protection, assuming that they are effective against countermeasures. Upper- and lower-tier defences will require detection and tracking probabilities above 0.94–0.97, and interceptor SSPKs above 0.5–0.6, if they are to handle attacks containing between 50 and 200 warheads. These are not unrealistic goals against relatively simple threats, although this level of performance has yet to be demonstrated in tests, and could be difficult to achieve in the presence of countermeasures.

Financial constraints are likely to mean that fewer TMD interceptors than planned are eventually deployed. This may be desirable because the large THAAD and NTW programmes currently envisioned could appear to be adjuncts to a US NMD system, thus threatening Russian and Chinese strategic missiles. To allay fears in Moscow and Beijing, the total number of deployed US upper-tier interceptors should be limited to between 600 and 800. An upper-tier defence with 800 interceptors, when combined with an equally capable lower tier, would still be able to defend against attacks containing up to 200 warheads, assuming that it can achieve the performance levels cited above. US cooperation on theatre defences with Taiwan and, possibly, Japan will be of greater concern to China. Beijing's reactions could have an adverse impact on many other US security concerns, and restraint in this area is therefore important. The hypothetical impact of a Russian upper-tier theatre defence on the retaliatory capabilities of the US, France and the UK is manageable, provided that no more than 500 'THAAD-like' interceptors are deployed. Again, however, the impact on China would be greater.

The main limitation of national and theatre systems which attempt to intercept missile warheads in their midcourse or terminal phases is that they are potentially vulnerable to countermeasures. However, relatively few countermeasures exist against boost-phase defences. Airborne interceptors launched from high-altitude UAVs may provide an effective and robust theatre *and* national missile defence against small states such as North Korea, Iraq and possibly Iran. Moreover, this type of defence would not pose a serious threat to Russian or Chinese strategic missiles because the UAVs would have to fly directly over these countries' airspace. Most would find it difficult to reach their orbit locations, would not last long against Russian and Chinese air defences if they did so, would be largely ineffective against salvo launches and could be attacked at the few airbases from which they originate. If Russia deploys its SLBMs into the open ocean, too many UAVs would be needed to maintain adequate coverage of all possible launch locations. None of these concerns pertains to small emerging ballistic-missile states, whose air defences tend to be weak and can be suppressed in the event of hostilities.

The principal drawback of airborne boost-phase systems is that they offer no protection against accidental or unauthorised Russian or Chinese missile launches. There are also technical and operational limitations that need to be examined in greater detail before the US could commit to these defences. Nevertheless, given that adverse international reactions to its current NMD plans could undermine US security in the long term, airborne (and naval) systems should be looked at more closely. Since airborne boost-phase missile defences pose very little threat to any of the five major nuclear powers, cooperative deployments could even be possible.

Appendix 1

Selected Ballistic-Missile Inventories and Characteristics

Missiles (by country)	Status/Initial operating capability[1]	Propellant type	Stages	Launchers	Missiles	Approximate range (km)	Approximate payload (kg)
Afghanistan							
Scud-B	mid-1980s; withdrawn 1999	liquid	1	0	0	280	985
Algeria							
Scud-B	operational	liquid	1	-	-	280	985
Argentina							
Condor-I	late 1970s	solid	1	-	-	100	400
Condor-II	cancelled	liquid	1	-	-	800/1,000	500
Armenia							
Scud-B	operational	liquid	1	-	-	280	985
Azerbaijan							
Scud-B	operational	liquid	1	-	-	280	985
Belarus							
SS-21	operational	solid	1	-	-	120	480
Scud-B	operational	liquid	1	60	-	280	985
Brazil							
SS-300/600	cancelled	liquid	1	-	-	300/600	500
MB/EE-350/-600/-1000	cancelled	liquid	1	-	-	300/600/1,000	500
Bulgaria							
Scud-B	operational	liquid	1	36	-	280	985
SS-23	operational	solid	1	8	8	500	450

Missiles (by country)	Status/Initial operating capability[1]	Propellant type	Stages	Launchers	Missiles	Approximate range (km)	Approximate payload (kg)
China							
DF-2/2A (CSS-1)	retired	liquid	1	-	-	1,250	1,500
DF-3/3A (CSS-2)	1971	liquid	1	60	50–80	2,650–2,800	2,150
DF-4 (CSS-3)	1980	liquid	2	10	20–30	4,750	2,200
DF-5/5A (CSS-4)	1981	liquid	2	~20	~20	12,000–13,000	3,200
DF-21/21A (CSS-5)	1986	solid	2	10	36–50	1,800	600
DF-15/M-9 (CSS-6)	1995	solid	1	-	200+	600	500–950
DF-11/M-11 (CSS-7)	1995	solid	2	-	40+	280	800
DF-25	cancelled	solid	2	-	-	1,700	2,000
JL-1 (CSS-N-3)	1986	solid	2	12–24	12–24	1,700	600
DF-31/JL-2	2003?	solid	3	-	-	8,000	700
DF-41	2010?	solid	3	-	-	12,000	800
DROC							
Scud-B	1999	liquid	1	-	-	280	985
Scud-C	1999	liquid	1	-	-	500	700
Czech Republic							
SS-21	operational	solid	1	-	-	120	480
Scud-B	retired	liquid	1	-	-	280	985
SS-23	retired	solid	1	-	-	500	450
Egypt							
Scud-B	early 1970s	liquid	1	9	100+	280	985
Scud-C	development?	liquid	1	-	-	450	985
Badr-2000	cancelled	solid	2	-	-	1,000	700
Georgia							
Scud-B	operational	liquid	1	-	-	280	985

Missiles (by country)	Status/ Initial operating capability[1]	Propellant type	Stages	Launchers	Missiles	Approximate range (km)	Approximate payload (kg)
Hungary							
SS-21	operational	solid	1	–	–	120	480
Scud-B	operational	liquid	1	–	–	280	985
India							
Prithvi 150	operational	liquid	1	–	25	150	1,000
Prithvi 250	operational	liquid	1	–	25	250	500
Prithvi 350	development	liquid	1	–	–	350	–
Agni 1	development	liquid/solid	2	–	–	1,500	1,000
Agni 2	development	solid	2	–	–	2,000	1,000
Sagarika SLBM	development	solid	–	–	–	300?	500?
Surya	development	liquid/solid	3	–	–	12,000	–
Iran							
M-7/CSS-8	operational	liquid/solid	2	~25	90–200	150	190
Scud-B[2]	1985	liquid	1	–	250–300	280–330	985
Scud-C[2]	1991	liquid	1	–	~200	500	700
Shahab-3	2000?	liquid	1	–	–	1,300	750
Shahab-4	development	liquid	1/2	–	–	2,000	1,000
Shahab-5	development	liquid	2	–	–	5,500	?
Iraq							
Ababeel-100 / *Al-Samoud*	development	liquid	1	–	–	100–150	300
Scud-B[2]	destroyed	liquid	1	–	–	280–330	985
Al-Hussayn	destroyed?	liquid	1	?	6–16[3]	600	500
Al-Abbas	destroyed	liquid	1	–	–	950	300
Al-Tammuz	destroyed	liquid	1	–	–	2,000	750

Missiles (by country)	Status/ Initial operating capability[1]	Propellant type	Stages	Launchers	Missiles	Approximate range (km)	Approximate payload (kg)
Israel							
Lance	operational	liquid	1	12	100–160	130	270
Jericho 1	early 1970s	solid	1	-	~50	500–750	500
Jericho 2	early 1990s	solid	1	-	~50	800	1,000
Jericho 2b	early 1990s	solid	1	-	-	1,300–1,500	1,000
Kazakstan							
SS-21	operational	solid	1	-	-	120	480
Scud-B	operational	liquid	1	-	<50	280	985
North Korea							
Frog-5	operational	solid	1	9	50	50	435
Frog-7	operational	solid	1	18	54	70	435
Scud-B[2]	early 1980s	liquid	1	12	<50	280–330	985
Scud-C[2]	1989	liquid	1	~30	<50	500	700
No-dong 1	1999	liquid	1	-	-	1,300	1,000
Taepo-dong 1	2000?	liquid	2	-	-	2,000	1,000
Taepo-dong 2	2003?	liquid	2	-	-	4,000–6,000	1,000
Taepo-dong 2/ICBM	2003?	liquid/solid	3	-	-	12,000	200–300
South Korea							
NHK-I	operational	solid	1	-	100	180	500
NHK-II	development	solid?	1	-	-	260	450
Libya							
Scud-B	1970s	liquid	1	80	<100	280	985
Al-Fatah	development	liquid	1	-	-	950	500

Missiles (by country)	Status/ Initial operating capability[1]	Propellant type	Stages	Launchers	Missiles	Approximate range (km)	Approximate payload (kg)
Pakistan							
Hatf 1	operational	solid	1	-	-	80	500
Hatf 2	operational	solid	1	-	-	280–330	500
Hatf 3/M-11	1995?	solid	2	-	30–80	280	800
Shaheen 1/Hatf 4?	development?	solid	1	-	-	800	500
Shaheen 2	development?	solid	2?	-	-	2,000	500
Ghauri 1/No-dong 1	1999?	liquid	1	-	~10	1,300	1,000
Ghauri 2/Taepo-dong 1	development?	liquid	2	-	-	2,000	1,000
Poland							
SS-21	operational	solid	1	-	-	120	480
Scud-B	operational	liquid	1	-	-	280	985
Romania							
Scud-B	operational	liquid	1	13	-	280	985
Saudi Arabia							
DF-3 (CSS-2)	operational	liquid	1	8–12	40–120	2,650	2,150
Slovakia							
SS-21	operational	solid	1	-	-	120	480
Scud-B	operational	liquid	1	-	-	280	985
SS-23	being retired	solid	1	-	10	500	450
South Africa							
Arniston	cancelled	liquid	1	-	-	1,450	1,000
Syria							
SS-21 Mod 2	1983	solid	1	-	-	120	480
Scud-B	early 1970s	liquid	1	24	100+	280	985
Scud-C	1991	liquid	1	12–24	50+	500	700
M-9/DF-15	purchased?	liquid	1	-	-	600	500

COLORADO COLLEGE LIBRARY
COLORADO SPRINGS
COLORADO

Missiles (by country)	Status/ Initial operating capability[1]	Propellant type	Stages	Launchers	Missiles	Approximate range (km)	Approximate payload (kg)
Taiwan							
Ching Feng (*Green Bee*)	operational?	liquid	1	-	-	130	400
Tien Ma (*Sky Horse*)	development?	liquid	1	-	-	950	500
Turkmenistan							
Scud-B	operational	liquid	1	-	<50	280	985
Ukraine							
SS-21	operational	solid	1	-	-	120	480
Scud-B	operational	liquid	1	-	<100	280	985
United Arab Emirates							
Scud-B	1989, not operational	liquid	1	6	-	280	985
Vietnam							
Scud-B	operational	liquid	1	-	<50	280	985
Yemen							
SS-21 Mod 2	operational	solid	1	12	24	120	480
Scud-B	operational	liquid	1	6	18	280	985
FRY							
Scud-B (modified)	operational?	liquid	1	-	-	400	700

Sources *The Nonproliferation Review*, vol. 4, no. 1, Autumn 1996, pp. 177–80; *Ballistic and Cruise Missile Threats*, NAIC-1031-0985-98 (Wright Patterson Air Force Base, OH: National Air Intelligence Center, 1998); Dov S. Zakheim, 'Old Rivalries, New Arsenals', *IEEE Spectrum*, March 1999, pp. 30–31; John Wilson Lewis and Hua Di, 'China's Ballistic Missile Programs: Technologies, Strategies, Goals', *International Security*, vol. 17, no. 2, Autumn 1992, pp. 9–11; Federation of American Scientists, www.fas.org/irp/threat/missile/index.html; and Joseph Cirincione, 'Assessing the Assessment: The 1999 National Intelligence Estimate of the Ballistic Missile Threat', *The Nonproliferation Review*, vol. 7, no. 1, Spring 2000, pp. 133–35.

Appendix 2

Future Strategic Nuclear Forces

This appendix describes possible strategic nuclear force structures for the US, Russia, China, France and the UK in 2010–15. Considerable uncertainty surrounds these projections because of economic constraints on modernising forces, and because the level of importance accorded to nuclear weapons is changing. Moreover, these force structures are based on current trends, and do not take into account the reactions that might follow the deployment of US missile defences.

The United States

The constraints imposed by a prospective START III treaty are the greatest unknown affecting the size of the future US strategic nuclear force. The following force is consistent with the ceiling of 2,500 strategic weapons announced at the US–Russian Helsinki Summit in March 1997. It is assumed to consist of 300 single-warhead ICBMs, 10% of which could survive a Russian first strike; 14 *Trident* SSBNs, each loaded with 20 D-5 SLBMs (instead of 24) carrying four warheads apiece, for a total SLBM force of 1,120 warheads; and a bomber force with 90 B-52Hs carrying 12 air-launched cruise missiles each, giving a total of 1,080 weapons. Half of the *Trident* submarines are assumed to be at sea in peacetime, and all but two on generated alert. Eighty per cent of the US bomber force is assumed to be on alert in a crisis, but none in peacetime, and each cruise missile has an 80% chance of penetrating Russia's airspace.

Russia

The bulk of Russia's existing force will become obsolete within the next seven years. Financial difficulties have forced the early retirement of some strategic systems, created maintenance problems for others and caused force modernisation to be delayed. Although the fate of START III is uncertain, Russia would in any case find it difficult to maintain forces above the level allowed by START II, unless it produced a new MIRVed ICBM the same size as the SS-19.

Three possible force structures are described below. All of them are slightly larger than the frequently quoted size of the future START III Russian force – between 1,000 and 1,500 strategic nuclear weapons – because the SS-27 (*Topol*-M) ICBM, a modernised version of the SS-25, is assumed to be allowed to carry three MIRVs.[1] The largest force contains 1,794 warheads, representing what could probably be deployed if the Russian economy recovers, and Russian leaders act according to their public statements and place a high priority on modernising the country's strategic nuclear forces.[2] It consists of 90 silo-based and 180 road-mobile *Topol*-Ms; ten new *Borey* SSBNs with 12 SS-NX-28 missiles, each carrying four warheads for a total of 480; and 24 *Bear*-H16 bombers carrying 16 AS-15 air-launched cruise missiles apiece, and ten *Blackjack* bombers with 12 AS-15s each (a total of 504 missiles).[3] This force size assumes that Russia retains only approximately half of the *Bears* that it possesses today, with preferential retention of the *Bear*-H16, and only ten of its 12 *Blackjack* bombers.[4] Bomber production, which ended in 1991, would have to resume around 2010 if Russia wants to keep a bomber force beyond 2015. Larger START III arsenals could be obtained if more *Topol*-Ms are deployed (estimates rarely exceed 900), more *Borey* submarines are produced, more than four warheads are deployed on each SS-NX-28, or more bombers are deployed.[5]

More modest economic recovery would produce a smaller force, assumed here to contain 1,428 warheads. This consists of 90 silo-based and 90 mobile *Topol*-Ms with three warheads each; eight *Borey* submarines loaded with 12 SS-NX-28 missiles each carrying four warheads (a total of 384 SLBM warheads); and 24 *Bear*-H16 bombers and ten *Blackjacks* carrying 504 AS-15 cruise missiles. If economic and political conditions continue to deteriorate, Russia may have a force containing only 1,161 warheads by 2010–15. This could comprise 60 silo-based and 60 mobile *Topol*-Ms with three warheads each; six *Boreys* carrying a total of 288 SLBM warheads; and, again, 24 *Bear*-H16 and ten *Blackjack* bombers carrying 504 AS-15 cruise missiles. Under START III, Russia could increase the size of its ballistic-missile force by between 270 and 1,000 warheads, depending on the exact force structure, by loading each missile with the maximum possible number of warheads.

On generated alert, only 10% of Russia's silo-based ICBMs are assumed to survive a US counterforce first strike, despite the Russian doctrinal preference for launching them before a US attack arrives. This represents a Russian worst-case perspective. Eighty-five per cent of Russia's mobile ICBMs are assumed to be out of their garrisons, 80% of SSBNs at sea and 80% of bombers on alert at dispersed airbases. Of the surviving bomber force, 60% is assumed to penetrate US air defences. This translates into a Russian retaliatory capability of approximately 805 warheads for the 1,428-warhead force on generated alert. Although these assumptions are plausible for a future Russian force, maintenance problems, personnel shortages and funding difficulties mean that today only about half of the current Strategic Rocket Forces can be brought to combat-alert status. On day-to-day alert, 10% of silo-based ICBMs are assumed to survive, two mobile regiments (18 missiles) are assumed to be out of garrison, two SSBNs at sea, and no bombers on alert. This gives a surviving day-to-day alert force of approximately 180 warheads. SSBNs are not credited with a launch-under-attack capability while they are at dockside, despite the fact that the Soviet Union practised such alerts during the Cold War.[6]

China

The future shape of China's nuclear force depends on the economic and technological resources available, Beijing's threat perceptions and China's commitment to international arms-control agreements. Although Chinese leaders emphasise economic growth over military modernisation, they remain committed to modernising the country's nuclear forces. Estimating the size of China's nuclear force between 2010 and 2015 is difficult because of the lack of information regarding modernisation plans.[7] China is thought to have enough fissile material to expand its arsenal from approximately 450 to between 600 and 900 weapons, although some estimates run as high as 2,700.[8]

China's long-range nuclear-strike capability is likely to increase substantially in the next decade. Two new mobile solid-fuel ICBMs are being developed: the DF-31, with a range estimated at 8,000km with a 700kg payload; and the DF-41, with an estimated range of 12,000km and a payload of 800kg.[9] A new solid-fuel SLBM based on the DF-31, the JL-2, is also being developed; 16 are expected to be deployed on each new Type 094 SSBN.[10] China's SSBN fleet could comprise between three and six submarines after 2010, giving rise to a sea-based deterrent with 48–96 missiles.[11] China has been working on MIRV technology since the early 1980s, but has yet to field a MIRVed ballistic missile.[12] The new-generation solid-fuel ICBMs and SLBMs will have smaller throw-weights than the older liquid-fuel missiles, making them less suitable for multiple warheads. Nevertheless, the DF-41 reportedly may carry up to three MIRVs.[13] No new medium-range bombers are being developed, although China appears committed to modernising its tactical air force with the addition of the nuclear-capable H-7 fighter-bomber.[14]

Thus, China's missile force in 2010–15 may contain eight DF-5 Mod 2 ICBMs, possibly carrying three MIRVs; 10–30 DF-41 ICBMs carrying one or more warheads; 20–40 single-warhead DF-31 ICBMs; 50–70 single-warhead DF-21 IRBMs; and 48–96 JL-2 single-warhead SLBMs aboard between three and six Type 094 SSBNs. Around ten H-6 medium bombers carrying one to three bombs each might still be in service.[15] The remainder of the bomber force will comprise tactical aircraft, possibly carrying up to 120 weapons, which do not pose a strategic threat to Russia. This equates to a future strategic nuclear force with 102–190 ballistic-missile warheads capable of reaching the US, and 162–290 ballistic-missile and aircraft weapons capable of reaching Russia. Currently, approximately 20 DF-5/5A ICBMs can reach US territory, most of which would not survive a US counterforce first strike.

The next generation of Chinese ICBMs and IRBMs will be solid-fuel, mobile missiles. Hence, they should survive US or Russian counterforce attacks better than the older DF-5/5A ICBMs (70% are assumed to survive). Moreover, a significant fraction (assumed here to be 50%) of the new Type 094 SSBNs might survive long enough to launch their missiles. As for China's ageing medium-range bomber fleet, only a third of the H-6 bombers are assumed to survive a Russian counterforce attack and penetrate Russian airspace. If China uses shorter-range H-7 bombers to attack Russia, this number could increase substantially, at least for attacks along the Russian periphery. No Chinese bombers have the range to strike the US.[16]

France

This analysis assumes that France can deploy at most four of its five *L'Inflexible*-class SSBNs to sea on generated alert since one is always in overhaul. Armed with the M4B SLBM, which carries six warheads, this gives France a survivable sea-based strategic force with around 384 warheads. The number of SSBNs will drop from five to four when the *Triomphant* class replaces the *L'Inflexible* submarines in around 2005, perhaps with a corresponding fall in the number of warheads. French ballistic missiles are believed to be able to carry penetration aids. The S3D IRBMs on the Plateau d'Albion have been retired. France might also have approximately 80 *Air-Sol, Moyenne Portée* (ASMP) weapons by 2015, carried aboard the *Mirage* IVP, *Mirage* 2000N and *Super Etendard* aircraft, only half of which are assumed to survive and penetrate Russian airspace. Modernisation plans include a longer-range *Air-Sol, Longue Portée* (ASLP) missile.

The United Kingdom

By 2015, the UK should be able to deploy three of its four *Vanguard*-class SSBNs to sea in a crisis. Each will carry 16 *Trident* D-5 ballistic missiles, probably armed with four warheads each, giving 64 warheads per submarine. The British government has, however, stated that its submarines can carry up to 96 warheads each.[17] These missiles are believed to carry penetration aids; the *Polaris Chevaline* missile reportedly deployed two sophisticated decoys for each of its two warheads, along with other penetration aids.[18] All British air-delivered nuclear weapons are retired. The UK's strategic deterrent on generated alert is thus assumed to consist of at least 192 survivable warheads by 2015.

Notes

Acknowledgements

The author would like to thank David Bernstein, George Bunn, Steve Fetter, Charles Glaser, Lieutenant-General Glenn Kent (US Air Force, retired), John Lewis, Michael May, Michel Oksenberg, Ted Postol and David Vaughan. Without the support of the Center for International Security and Cooperation, Stanford University, and the Carnegie Corporation, this work would not have been possible. The views expressed here are solely the author's, and do not reflect those of the Center, the Carnegie Corporation or any of the Center's other sponsors.

Definitions

This paper uses the following standard ballistic-missile designations: short-range ballistic missile (SRBM) for ballistic missiles with a range of less than 1,000 kilometres; medium-range ballistic missile (MRBM) for ranges between 1,000km and 3,000km; intermediate-range ballistic missile (IRBM) for ranges between 3,000km and 5,500km; and intercontinental ballistic missile (ICBM) for ranges beyond 5,500km. Submarine-launched ballistic missiles (SLBMs) have medium to intercontinental ranges.

Chapter 1

[1] Ballistic-missile payloads are typically between 500 kilograms and 1,000kg. Attack times are approximately four minutes for 300km-range missiles, up to more than 30 minutes for ICBMs or SLBMs with ranges of over 9,000km. Accuracy is typically 0.5–2km circular error probable for missiles with ranges below 1,000km, and 2–4km for missiles with ranges of between 1,000km and 3,000km.
[2] See Steve Rodan, 'Iran Now Able to Deploy Shahab-3', *Jane's Defence Weekly*, 22 March 2000, p. 15.
[3] Bill Gertz, 'N. Korean Missile Seen Posing Risk to US', *Washington Times*, 16 September 1998, p. 1; Gus

Constantine, 'N. Korean Satellite Described as a Dud', *ibid.*, 11 September 1998, p. 17; and David Wright, 'Taepodong 1 Test Flight', Federation of American Scientists, 2 September 1998, www.fas.org/news/dprk/1998/980831-dprk-dcw.htm.

[4] See Steven J. Isakowitz, Joseph P. Hopkins Jr. and Joshua B. Hopkins, *International Reference Guide to Space Launch Systems*, Third Edition (Reston, VA: American Institute of Aeronautics and Astronautics (AIAA), 1999), pp. xii–xvi.

[5] See US General Accounting Office (USGAO), *Foreign Missile Threats: Analytic Soundness of Certain National Intelligence Estimates*, GAO/NSIAD-96-225, August 1996, p. 3.

[6] Donald H. Rumsfeld *et al.*, *Executive Summary of the Report of the Commission to Assess the Ballistic Missile Threat to the United States*, 15 July 1998, www.fas.org/irp/threat/missile/rumsfeld/index.html.

[7] *Ibid.*, pp. 4–5, 7–8, 14–23; and Bill Gertz, 'Russia, China Aid Iran's Missile Program', *Washington Times*, 10 September 1997, p. 1.

[8] See Robert D. Walpole, *Foreign Missile Developments and the Ballistic Missile Threat to the United States Through 2015*, National Intelligence Council, September 1999, www.fas.org/irp/threat/missile/nie99msl.htm.

[9] The Rumsfeld Commission report stated that the *Taepo-dong* 2 might have a range of 10,000km with a reduced payload. See Rumsfeld *et al.*, *Executive Summary*, p. 9. Walpole, *Foreign Missile Developments* (p. 2), stated that a three-stage *Taepo-dong* 2 is a more likely candidate for a North Korean ICBM with a payload of several hundred kilograms.

[10] *Ibid.*, pp. 10–11; and Kenneth R. Timmerman, *Russian Assistance to Iran's Missile Programs*, Testimony before the Subcommittee on Space and Aeronautics of the Committee on Science, US House of Representatives, Washington DC, 13 July 1999.

[11] See Rumsfeld *et al.*, *Executive Summary*, pp. 11–12.

[12] See Walpole, *Foreign Missile Developments*, p. 2.

[13] For a discussion of the role of nuclear weapons in deterring chemical and biological attacks, see David Gompert, Kenneth Watman and Dean Wilkening, 'Nuclear First Use Revisited', *Survival*, vol. 37, no. 3, Autumn 1995, pp. 27–44; and Scott D. Sagan, 'The Commitment Trap: Why the United States Should Not Use Nuclear Threats to Deter Biological and Chemical Weapons Attacks', *International Security*, vol. 24, no. 4, Spring 2000, pp. 85–115.

[14] Iraq's fixed *Scud* launch sites, unlike its mobile launchers, were largely destroyed within the first few minutes of the 1991 Gulf War (private communication, Timothy McCarthy, Center for Non-Proliferation Studies, Monterey Institute for International Studies, Monterey, CA). See also Barry D. Watts and Thomas A. Keany, *Gulf War Air Power Survey, Volume II: Effects and Effectiveness* (Washington DC: US Government Printing Office (USGPO), 1993), pp. 333–34.

[15] See Bill Gertz, 'Russian Renegades Pose Nuke Danger', *Washington Times*, 22 October 1996, p. 1.

[16] Walpole, *Foreign Missile Developments*, p. 8.

[17] See remarks made by Robert D. Walpole, Carnegie Endowment for International Peace, Washington DC, 17 September 1998,

www.ceip.org/programs/npp/walpole.htm.

[18] For a good treatment of Soviet/Russian nuclear command-and-control, see Bruce Blair, *The Logic of Accidental Nuclear War* (Washington DC: The Brookings Institution, 1993), chap. 4.

[19] In principle, an unauthorised attack from a single Russian ICBM launch-control centre could involve up to ten missiles, depending on the silo complex, or up to nine for an SS-25 battalion. This would produce attacks with up to ten warheads, or possibly up to 30 if the SS-27 (*Topol*-M) carries three MIRVs. If the codes required to launch SLBMs can be circumvented, as many as 16 or 20 might be launched, carrying a total of between 48 and 200 warheads.

[20] During the attempted coup in Russia in 1991, senior field commanders responsible for the country's nuclear forces apparently formed a secret pact to disobey any nuclear launch orders given by the coup plotters. See Blair, *The Logic of Accidental Nuclear War*, pp. 65–66.

[21] Launching Russian missiles before US missiles arrive on target in a counterforce attack is an option Russian strategic planners have considered for years. Traditional Soviet writings on the subject emphasised large, prompt responses, involving the bulk of the Soviet silo-based ICBM force and SLBMs on pier-side alert. Stephen Meyer, 'Soviet Nuclear Operations', in Ashton B. Carter, John D. Steinbruner and Charles A. Zraket (eds), *Managing Nuclear Operations* (Washington DC: The Brookings Institution, 1987); and Bruce Blair, *Global Zero Alert for Nuclear Forces* (Washington DC: The Brookings Institution, 1995).

[22] For a proposal calling for de-alerting nuclear forces, see Blair, *Global Zero Alert*; for how ballistic missiles might be destroyed after launch, see Sherman Frankel, 'Aborting Unauthorized Launches of Nuclear-Armed Ballistic Missiles through Post-Launch Destruction', *Science and Global Security*, vol. 2, 1990, pp. 1–20.

[23] Jonathan Tucker and Timothy McCarthy, 'Saddam's Toxic Arsenal: Chemical and Biological Weapons and Missiles in the Gulf Wars', in Peter Lavoy, Scott D. Sagan and James Wirtz (eds), *Planning the Unthinkable: New Powers and the Use of Nuclear, Chemical, and Biological Weapons* (Ithaca, NY: Cornell University Press, forthcoming 2000).

[24] See George Quester and Victor Utgoff, 'No-First-Use and Non-proliferation: Redefining Extended Deterrence', *Washington Quarterly*, vol. 17, no. 2, Spring 1994, p. 107.

[25] Unofficial translation of the *Federal Law on Ratification of the Treaty Between the Russian Federation and the United States of America on Further Reductions and Limitation of Strategic Offensive Arms*, PIR Arms Control Letters, 2, Center for Policy Studies in Russia, 14 April 2000.

[26] See Giles Whittell, 'Russia Dusts Off Nuclear Plan', *The Times*, 14 October 1999, p. 21; and David Hoffman, 'New Russian Security Plan Criticizes West', *Washington Post*, 15 January 2000, p. 1.

[27] For a more detailed discussion, see Dean A. Wilkening, 'Amending the ABM Treaty', *Survival*, vol. 42, no. 1, Spring 2000, pp. 29–45.

[28] See David S. Yost, 'Ballistic Missile Defense and the Atlantic Alliance', *International Security*, vol. 7, no. 2, Autumn 1982, pp. 143–74.

[29] On Chinese views, see Ambassador Sha Zukang, 'US Missile Defense Plans: China's

View', *Disarmament Diplomacy*, no. 43, January–February 2000, p. 3.

[30] Michael C. Sirak, 'United States, Japan Finalize Deal on Navy Theater Wide Cooperation', *Inside Missile Defense*, vol. 5, no. 17, 25 August 1999, p. 12.

[31] On Chinese naval strategy for a blockade of Taiwan, see John W. Lewis and Xue Litai, *China's Strategic Seapower: Politics of Force Modernization in the Nuclear Age* (Stanford, CA: Stanford University Press, 1994), pp. 227–28.

[32] China's past response to US and Russian ABM systems was to deploy penetration aids. Developing MIRVs was also considered, but was delayed due to the lack of a lightweight warhead and technical hurdles associated with the post-boost vehicle. See John Wilson Lewis and Hua Di, 'China's Ballistic Missile Programs: Technologies, Strategies, Goals', *International Security*, vol. 17, no. 2, Autumn 1992, pp. 21–22; James A. Lamson and Wyn Q. Bowen, '"One Arrow, Three Stars": China's MIRV Program, Part I', *Jane's Intelligence Review*, May 1997, pp. 216–18; and James A. Lamson and Wyn Q. Bowen, '"One Arrow, Three Stars": China's MIRV Program, Part II', *ibid.*, June 1997, pp. 266–69.

[33] US Arms Control and Disarmament Agency (ACDA), *Second Agreed Statement Relating to the Treaty Between the United States of America and the Union of Soviet Socialist Republics on the Limitation of Anti-Ballistic Missile Systems of May 26, 1972* (Washington DC: ACDA, 26 September 1997).

[34] The BMDO's performance criterion for NMD is a '95 percent confidence of a 95 percent kill probability' assuming four interceptors are fired at each incoming object in shoot-look-shoot mode, with two shots fired in the first shot opportunity and two in the second. This is equivalent to a probability of 0.82 that no warhead leaks through the defence for attacks containing up to ten warheads. See Michael Dornheim, 'Missile Defense Design Juggles Complex Factors', *Aviation Week and Space Technology*, 24 February 1997, p. 54.

[35] PAC-3 flight tests in March 1999, September 1999 and February 2000 succeeded; THAAD flight tests in June and August 1999 were also successful; and the first NMD interceptor test in October 1999 hit its target. The kill vehicle tested in January 2000 missed its target.

[36] Relatively little has been written about BMD countermeasures and counter-countermeasures. References include: Richard L. Garwin and Hans A. Bethe, 'Anti-Ballistic Missile Systems', *Scientific American*, March 1968; Nicholas Bloembergen *et al.*, 'Acquisition, Tracking, and Discrimination', American Physical Society Study Group Report on the Science and Technology of Directed Energy Weapons, Reviews of Modern Physics, vol. 59, no. 3, Part II, July 1987, pp. 145–68; Uzi Rubin and Azriel Lorber, 'Future Trend of Missile Proliferation in the Middle East and Its Impact on Regional Missile Defence', paper presented at the 1995 AIAA conference on theatre-missile defence, London; Andrew M. Sessler *et al.*, *Countermeasures: A Technical Evaluation of the Operational Effectiveness of the Planned US National Missile Defense System*, Union of Concerned Scientists and MIT Security Studies Program, April 2000, www.ucsusa.org/arms/CM_exec.html.

[37] See Sherman Frankel, 'Guest

Perspective: Electronic Decoys to Defeat Missile Defense Systems', *Inside Missile Defense*, vol. 5, no. 9, 5 May 1999, pp. 25–26.

[38] Exoatmospheric intercepts occur at altitudes above approximately 80–100km; endoatmospheric ones take place below this altitude. This distinction is important principally because simple lightweight decoys such as balloons and chaff are removed from the 'threat cloud' due to atmospheric drag at altitudes of between 80km and 100km, thus making decoy discrimination easier for endoatmospheric intercepts.

[39] See Dornheim, 'Missile Defense Design Juggles Complex Factors', p. 54. For an estimate of the THAAD SSPK equal to 0.80, see 'THAAD', *World Missiles Briefing* (Fairfax, VA: Teal Group Corporation, 1996), p. 6. Using the NMD performance criterion stated by the BMDO, it can be inferred that NMD interceptor SSPKs must be above 0.65.

[40] See Michael C. Sirak, 'In NMD Test, Beacon Will Help Position EKV until Booster Release', *Inside Missile Defense*, vol. 5, no. 9, 5 May 1999, p. 20.

[41] According to one assessment, modest trajectory shaping, simple exoatmospheric decoys or chaff, missiles or missile warheads which intentionally perform barrel-roll manoeuvres within the atmosphere, and low-power electronic countermeasures against radar-guided homing interceptors may be possible for emerging ballistic-missile states by 2010. However, more sophisticated decoys that mimic the radars and infra-red signatures of re-entry vehicles, 'stealthy' missiles or re-entry vehicles, sophisticated endoatmospheric manoeuvring,

electronic countermeasures against ground-based radars and multiple warheads are deemed to be beyond the technical capability of emerging ballistic-missile states, at least those in the Middle East. See Rubin and Lorber, 'Future Trend of Missile Proliferation in the Middle East'.

[42] Walpole, *Foreign Missile Developments* (p. 3), stated that Russia and China 'probably will sell some related [countermeasure] technologies' in the future.

[43] See Michael C. Sirak, 'DOD, Industry: NMD Countermeasures Getting Attention', *Inside Missile Defense*, vol. 5, no. 10, 19 May 1999, p. 1.

[44] See Michael C. Sirak, 'BMDO Director Says NMD System Prepared for Countermeasures', *ibid.*, vol. 6, no. 4, 23 February 2000, p. 1.

Chapter 2

[1] See Michael C. Sirak, 'NMD Officials Face Task To Merge Radars, Current Warning System', *Inside Missile Defense*, vol. 5, no. 22, 3 November 1999, pp. 14–16.

[2] Walter B. Slocombe, Testimony before the House Armed Services Committee, Hearing on National Missile Defence, 13 October 1999, www.house.gov/hasc/testimony/106thcongress/99-10-13slocombe.htm.

[3] See Michael C. Sirak, 'BMDO: NMD "C3" Architecture Could Feature Up To Nine X-band Radars', *Inside Missile Defense*, vol. 5, no. 10, 19 May 1999, pp. 13–14.

[4] See Michael C. Sirak, 'Favorable Winds, Seas Called Crucial To NMD Construction Process', *ibid.*, vol. 6, no. 7, 5 April 2000, p. 1.

[5] Two independent studies chaired by General Larry Welch have

warned of the high risk of failure associated with the fast pace at which NMD technologies are being pushed. See Larry Welch *et al.*, *Reducing Risk in Ballistic Missile Defense Flight Test Programs*, Federation of American Scientists, 27 February 1998; and *National Missile Defense Review*, Federation of American Scientists, 16 November 1999, as reproduced at www.fas.org/spp/starwars/ program/index.html.

[6] Michael C. Sirak, 'BMDO Plans Only One Production Decision on NMD Interceptor', *Inside Missile Defense*, vol. 6, no. 7, 5 April 2000, p. 14.

[7] Integrated Flight Test number 15 (IFT-15), currently planned for 2003, and IFT-18, currently planned for 2004, are designed to test 'threat-representative targets'. IFTs 14, 16 and 17 are designed to verify the lethality of the NMD kinetic-kill vehicle. Michael C. Sirak, 'BMDO Plans Two NMD Flight Tests with Special Threat-Like Targets', *ibid.*, vol. 5, no. 24, 1 December 1999, pp. 10–11.

[8] See Lieutenant-General Lester L. Lyles, Director, BMDO, 'Statement before the Senate Appropriations Committee, Subcommittee on Defense', 14 April 1999.

[9] These cost estimates are for then-year dollars, using a 2.5% inflator for operating and support costs. *Budgetary and Technical Implications of the Administration's Plan for National Missile Defense* (Washington DC: Congressional Budget Office, April 2000), p. 10.

[10] The range at which a target can be detected depends on its signature (the radar cross-section and/or infra-red signature), the technical performance and location of the sensors, and the number of incoming warheads that must be tracked simultaneously.

[11] In a barrage-firing doctrine, several interceptors are fired at the incoming target nearly simultaneously. In shoot-look-shoot mode, the defence initially fires one or two interceptors at each target, then a volley at any target that gets through. See Russell Shaver, 'Priorities for Ballistic Missile Defense', in Paul Davis (ed.), *New Challenges for Defense Planning: Rethinking How Much Is Enough* (Santa Monica, CA: RAND, 1994), pp. 280–81.

[12] See Dean A. Wilkening, 'A Simple Model for Calculating Ballistic Missile Defense Effectiveness', *Science and Global Security*, vol. 8, no. 2, 2000, pp. 183–215.

[13] For a barrage-firing doctrine, the number of shots taken at each warhead is constant along each of the interceptor contour lines. Thus, for example, four shots are taken at each target along the 20-interceptor contour line in Figure 1.

[14] The assumption that all interceptors can engage the incoming attack corresponds to a single-site nationwide defence, or a multi-site defence where the attack is spread uniformly throughout all defended areas. If an attack is concentrated on a subset of the defended areas in a multi-site defence, the number of interceptors that must be deployed is equal to the ratio S/N times the numbers given in Figure 1, where S is the number of sites required for complete coverage, and N the number of sites that can engage the incoming attack.

[15] This is true for barrage-firing doctrines and, with some restrictions, for shoot-look-shoot ones as well. See Wilkening, 'A

Simple Model', pp. 206–209.

[16] *Budgetary and Technical Implications of the Administration's Plan for National Missile Defense,* p. 12.

[17] History provides some clues as to the level of nuclear asymmetry required for coercive leverage in a crisis. In the 1962 Cuban missile crisis, the US had a six-to-one advantage over the Soviet Union in deployed strategic nuclear weapons. Counterforce attacks might have yielded more than a ten-to-one advantage in effective strategic nuclear capability. President Kennedy apparently did not believe that this provided much coercive leverage because an airstrike to destroy Soviet missiles in Cuba was rejected for fear that the crisis could escalate. See Scott Sagan, *Moving Targets: Nuclear Strategy and National Security* (Princeton, NJ: Princeton University Press, 1989), pp. 30–32.

[18] China's DF-5 ICBM reportedly carries light exoatmospheric decoys and electronic countermeasures, but no heavy endoatmospheric decoys. See John Wilson Lewis and Hua Di, 'China's Ballistic Missile Programs', p. 21.

[19] See David S. Yost, 'Nuclear Debates in France', *Survival*, vol. 36, no. 4, Winter 1994–95, pp. 113–39; and Nicholas K. J. Witney, 'British Nuclear Policy after the Cold War', *ibid.*, pp. 96–112.

Chapter 3

[1] 'Cost of Patriot Missile Increases $2.3 Billion', *Washington Post*, 14 April 2000, p. 7.

[2] Peter J. Skibitski, 'Navy Again Slides Date of First Area Anti-Ballistic Missile Flight Test', *Inside Missile Defense,* vol. 6, no. 6, 22 March 2000, p. 7.

[3] David Hughes, 'Navy Readies Fleet for Anti-Scud Warfare', *Aviation Week and Space Technology,* 24 February 1997, pp. 61–63; 'Navy Tactical Missile Defense', *World Missiles Briefing*; and John Pike, 'Ballistic Missile Defense: Is the US "Rushing to Failure"?', *Arms Control Today*, vol. 28, no. 3, April 1998, p. 11.

[4] Joseph Anselmo, 'MEADS Faces Tough Sell', *Aviation Week and Space Technology*, 3 March 1997, p. 57.

[5] Michael Dornheim, 'Thaad Program Future Tied to Test Results', *ibid.*, pp. 64–65.

[6] Michael Dornheim, 'Missile Defense Soon, But Will It Work?', *ibid.*, 24 February 1997, p. 39; and Pike, 'Ballistic Missile Defense'.

[7] Michael C. Sirak, 'BMDO Says THAAD To Be Fielded in FY-07, Navy System in FY-10 or Earlier', *Inside Missile Defense*, vol. 6, no. 3, 9 February 2000, p. 1.

[8] 'Navy Tactical Missile Defense', *World Missiles Briefing*; and Dornheim, 'Missile Defense Soon'.

[9] Michael Dornheim, '"Theater Wide" Missile Defense: Appealing, Controversial, Difficult', *Aviation Week and Space Technology*, 3 March 1997, pp. 62–63.

[10] Michael C. Sirak, 'BMDO Says THAAD To Be Fielded'.

[11] Department of Defense, *Report to Congress on Theater Missile Defense Architecture Options for the Asia-Pacific Region*, May 1999, www.fas.org/spp/starwars/program/tmd050499.htm.

[12] Dornheim, '"Theater Wide" Missile Defense', p. 62; and Department of Defense, *Report to Congress*.

[13] Boost-phase, upper-tier and lower-tier TMD layers can be

treated as nearly statistically independent, provided separate surveillance and tracking sensors support each layer. Common mode errors between layers must occur less than approximately 0.1% of the time for the analysis in this paper to remain valid.

[14] See Dornheim, 'Missile Defense Design Juggles Complex Factors'; 'THAAD', *World Missiles Briefing*, p. 6.

[15] An estimate of 2–4 hours for the nominal *Scud* reload time is given by Thomas Cochran, William Arkin, Robert Norris and Jeffrey Sands, *Nuclear Weapons Databook, Vol. IV: Soviet Nuclear Weapons* (New York: Natural Resources Defense Council, 1989), p. 221.

[16] See Duncan Lennox, 'Inside the R-17 "Scud B" Missile', *Jane's Intelligence Review*, vol. 3, no. 7, July 1991, p. 302; and David C. Isby, 'The Residual Iraqi "Scud" Force', *ibid.*, vol. 7, no. 3, July 1995, pp. 115–17.

[17] See Tucker and McCarthy, 'Saddam's Toxic Arsenal'; and Watts and Keany, *Gulf War Air Power Survey, Summary Report*, vol. 1, part 2, pp. 84–87.

[18] The total number of interceptors that must be deployed to a theatre to defend against concentrated attacks can be calculated by multiplying the number of interceptors given in Figures 5–7 by $(S+M-1)/M$, where S is the number of theatre-defence sites required for complete coverage, and M the number of theatre-ballistic missiles per mobile launcher in the arsenal.

[19] *The Future of Theater Missile Defense* (Washington DC: Congressional Budget Office, June 1994), p. 55; and Lisbeth Gronlund *et al.*, 'Highly Capable Theater Missile Defenses and the ABM

Treaty', *Arms Control Today*, vol. 24, no. 3, April 1994, pp. 3–8.

[20] *The Future of Theater Missile Defense*, p. 60.

[21] In this case, the assumption that the single-engagement THAAD footprint accurately reflects the defended area is not very good because each THAAD battery must potentially defend against hundreds of warheads simultaneously.

[22] ACDA, *Second Agreed Statement*.

Chapter 4

[1] During the 1991 Gulf War, for example, mobile *Scud* launchers were confined to less than one-quarter of Iraq's territory. See Watts and Keaney, *Gulf War Air Power Survey, Volume II*, p. 400.

[2] Richard L. Garwin, 'The Wrong Plan', *Bulletin of the Atomic Scientists*, vol. 56, no. 2, March–April 2000, pp. 39–41.

[3] Gigi Whitley, 'Commitment to Space-Based Laser More Critical than Exact Launch Date', *Inside Missile Defense*, vol. 5, no. 5, 10 March 1999, p. 25; and 'Key Senator Eager for Air Force to Begin Design of Space-Based Laser', *ibid.*, p. 27.

[4] David Mulholland, 'Global Hawk, DarkStar Offer Strategic Promise', *Defense News*, 14–20 September 1998, p. 16; and Peter Grier, 'DarkStar and Its Friends', *Air Force Magazine*, July 1996, p. 43.

[5] Michael C. Sirak, 'Israel Prepares to Offer Proposals for Next Phase of UAV-BPI Program', *Inside Missile Defense*, vol. 5, no. 4, 24 February 1999, p. 7.

[6] These are the range estimates for punching a hole in the booster's side, thereby causing booster

venting. Estimates for the maximum range for a more catastrophic booster failure are shorter: 240km for the *Scud*-B, 320km for the *Scud*-C and 185km for the *No-dong*. Geoffrey Forden, *The Airborne Laser: Shooting Down What's Going Up*, CISAC Working Paper (Stanford, CA: Center for International Security and Arms Control, September 1997).
[7] See Michael Ruane, 'US Looks to Lasers To Destroy Missiles', *Philadelphia Inquirer*, 8 April 1997, p. 1; and George Seffers, 'Some USAF Officials Predict Limits on Airborne Laser Role', *Defense News*, 18–24 November 1996, p. 8.
[8] Forden, *The Airborne Laser*, pp. 14–15.
[9] The actual number of footprints may be higher because the *Topol*-M is reported to have a shorter burn time than the *Topol* (SS-25) ICBM. See Nikolai Sokov, *Modernization of Strategic Nuclear Weapons in Russia: The Emerging New Posture*, Working Paper 6 (Cambridge, MA: Program on New Approaches to Russian Security, Davis Center for Russian Studies, Harvard University, May 1998), p. 34.

Appendix 1

[1] The status and/or date of the initial operating capability for a given missile deployment is often uncertain.
[2] The characteristics of *Scud*-Bs and *Scud*-Cs can differ between countries, depending on whether the missiles are of original Russian design, or have been modified for indigenous production.
[3] Iraq may have hidden 12–20 *Al-Hussayn* launchers and possibly as many as 100–200 *Al-Hussayn*

missiles from UN inspectors. Isby, 'The Residual Iraqi "Scud" Force', pp. 115–17.

Appendix 2

[1] The SS-25 ICBM was once tested with three warheads. A report in February 2000 by a prominent group of Russians suggested that the *Topol*-M could carry three or four MIRVs. See Sergei Karaganov and Yuli Vorontsov, *Russian–American Relations at the Turn of the Century*, Report of the Council on Foreign and Defence Policy Working Group on US–Russian Relations, February 2000, www.ceip.org/programs/ruseuras/usrus/contents.htm.
[2] Michael R. Gordon, 'Putin Vows Russia Will Reinvigorate Its Nuclear Force', *New York Times*, 1 April 2000, p. 1.
[3] By 2007, all of Russia's SS-18s, SS-19s, SS-24s and SS-25s will either be obsolete or must be destroyed according to START II. The future ICBM force mostly depends on the size of the *Topol*-M force.
[4] The size of the future Russian bomber force is uncertain. Until recently, Russia had a long-range aviation force with 57 *Bear*-H bombers and six *Blackjacks*. In October 1999, it received three *Bear*-Hs and eight *Blackjacks* from Ukraine. David Hoffman, 'Ukraine To Transfer 11 Bombers to Russia To Repay Part of Debt', *Washington Post*, 2 November 1999, p. 22.
[5] See Robert Holzer, 'US Study: Russia, China Sub Production Flourishes', *Defense News*, 24 February–2 March 1997, p. 8. A maximum of ten warheads, instead of 12, has been assumed for the SS-NX-28 because it is believed to be a

follow-on SLBM to the solid-fuel SS-N-20 (which carried ten warheads). If the SS-NX-28 carries 12 warheads, Russia could not deploy more than nine *Borey* submarines and remain compliant with the START II level of 1,750 SLBM warheads.

[6] For Russian day-to-day alert practices, see Bruce Blair, *Dealerting Strategic Forces* (Washington DC: The Brookings Institution, 1997).

[7] China's current strategic nuclear force contains approximately 20 DF-5/5A ICBMs; 20 DF-4s, 40 DF-3/3As and 48 DF-21 IRBMs; one *Xia* SSBN, which rarely leaves port, carrying 12 JL-1 SLBMs; and around 150 bombs aboard H-6, H-5 and Q-5 medium-range aircraft. Not counting the 12 SLBMs on the *Xia* submarine, only the DF-5/5A ICBMs can threaten the US. See Robert S. Norris, Andrew Burrows and Richard Fieldhouse, *Nuclear Weapons Databook, Vol. V, British, French, and Chinese Nuclear Weapons* (Boulder, CO: Westview Press, 1994), p. 359; and Robert S. Norris and William M. Arkin, 'Chinese Nuclear Forces, 1999', *Bulletin of the Atomic Scientists*, vol. 55, no. 3, May–June 1999, pp. 79–80.

[8] Alastair Iain Johnston, 'Prospects for Chinese Nuclear Force Modernization: Limited Deterrence Versus Multilateral Arms Control', *China Quarterly*, no. 146, June 1996, p. 562; and Ming Zhang, *China's Changing Nuclear Posture: Reactions to the South Asian Nuclear Tests* (Washington DC: Carnegie Endowment for International Peace, 1999), pp. 2, 83.

[9] See John Wilson Lewis and Hua Di, 'China's Ballistic Missile Programs', pp. 9–11.

[10] *Worldwide Submarine Challenges* (Washington DC: US Office of Naval Intelligence, February 1997), p. 22.

[11] *Ibid.*, p. 23; and Johnston, 'Prospects for Chinese Nuclear Force Modernization', p. 562.

[12] Lamson and Bowen, '"One Arrow, Three Stars": China's MIRV Program, Part I', p. 266.

[13] *Ibid.*, p. 268.

[14] See Norris, Burrows and Fieldhouse, *Nuclear Weapons Databook, Vol. V*, p. 373.

[15] The H-7 is the only modern Chinese bomber under construction. It is likely to be reserved for theatre missions. See *ibid.*, p. 368.

[16] *Ibid.*, pp. 358–96.

[17] *Ibid.*, pp. 100–20.

[18] *Ibid.*, pp. 105–13.